W9-CZX-720

the no significant difference phenomenon

compiled by
Thomas L. Russell

as reported in 355 research reports,

summaries, and papers

a comparative research annotated bibliography

on technology for distance education

A web site has been
established to maintain a
place for the posting of
additional NSD entries
found after the printing
of this book.
http:tenb.mta.ca/phenom/

no — significant — difference

contents

fore-word

Bloodletting, Media and Learning
Richard E. Clark

This book by Tom Russell is one of the few rational sources of information about an otherwise irrational and commercialized issue. He provides an abundance of evidence for an elegant, simple and empirically accurate point that has been advanced by a number of researchers in the past 70 years. The point is that no matter who or what is being taught, more than one medium will produce adequate learning results and we must choose the less expensive media or waste limited educational resources. His evidence base for the argument is the hundreds (some say thousands) of media comparison studies produced since the 1920's. Most of these studies comparing the learning benefits of different media have resulted in no significant differences. Yet the research has been largely ignored and disputed by three generations of educators and media specialists. Why?

Robert Heinich, a former professor at Indiana University and a long-time editor of "Audio Visual Communication Review" (now called "Educational Technology Research and Development") viewed this argument as a conflict between separate economic interests. Bob thought that the reason for the dispute could be found in the political and economic conflicts between K-12 classroom educators and university faculty on the one hand, and media advocates, including big media business, on the other hand. He noticed the large number of NSD dissertations and articles submitted to the journal over the years. He also noticed the smaller number of significant difference studies which tended to favor either classroom instruction or newer media, depending on who had designed or conducted the study. He suggested that both educators and media interests had economic, political and personal reasons for a stake in the outcome of comparative research.

Bob was the originator of the "John Henry Effect" in research design. Essentially, the John Henry Effect happens in an experiment where the "threatened comparison group" works harder to teach when they realized that their instruction was being compared with a competing media. Bob argued that many of the NSD (and a few significant) findings in media comparison studies were due to the John Henry Effect. If he was correct, then we could improve learning enormously if we were more motivated to do our best instructional job, no matter what media we are using.

What does it mean when we find "no significant differences" (NSD) in an adequately designed study? In science, NSD is an important finding, as important in every way as statistical significance. In fact, one might argue that one of the main contributions of science is to help us overcome our strong inclination only to accept evidence that confirms our beliefs about the world. In a rational world, a number of NSD findings would eventually lead us to change our views about the learning benefits of any particular medium. If medicine had ignored the NSD results of their research, we would still be arguing about whether bloodletting by leeches or knives was more effective for curing illnesses. While empirical method was primitive at that time, NSD results were ignored and arguments were advanced about the design of the knife or the way it was held, or about the species of leeches used and the location of the incision. The eventual solution for medicine was to find that bloodletting did not work regardless of the instrument, and so bloodletting was gradually discarded. This is different than the current argument about "managed care" in medicine. Some of those who argue about managed health care suggest that it leads to a serious reduction in the quality and results of patient recovery. The argument Russell advances is that when learning (or health) results are equivalent, we can get equal benefit from all compared providers.

The NSD media finding in studies where adequate learning occurs can be interpreted to mean that compared treatments are equal in their impact on learning. If the amount of learning produced by different media is similar (NSD) but adequate to meet our instructional goals, then all treatments are equally valuable for learning but will usually differ in their cost and convenience. Unlike bloodletting research, students do generally experience enough learning when the underlying design of all compared treatments is adequate. So, education must adopt the less expensive media - provided that learning outcomes are equivalent. Why spend more for instruction if there is a significantly less expensive way to achieve the same result? This is the very reasonable mood of the taxpayers and some of those who make our laws and manage our schools.

Yet, this view may be threatening to those who develop, advocate and sell newer media. I was one of those people 30 years ago when I left a commercial career in media to return to the university for a doctorate in education. I was very clear in my own mind that new media (television at that time) were going to revolutionize education and increase learning benefits for everyone. My own conversion to a different point of view developed gradually after reviewing earlier publications like Tom Russell's. Each of my arguments about the inadequate design of media research and the John Henry Effect and the bias of journal editors was eliminated with study and reflection. I arrived only reluctantly at the argument I advanced 15 years later, in the 1983 "Journal of Educational Research" article that Tom Russell mentions in his introduction.

———

Tom Russell's book is a reminder to all of us that our field has not been afflicted with rationality. His contribution to the dialogue has been considerable. He challenges all of us not to continually reinvent the wheel when making this argument. Read the literature that he describes and you will find that most of the arguments being voiced have been thoroughly examined and have not changed the NSD interpretation. Maybe someone reading this book will find a new argument. All of us are open to that eventuality. Those readers who are inclined to find a new point of view are reminded however that new insights happen to the prepared mind.

———

Progress requires that we move on to new arguments and directions. Perhaps that is why Tom has decided that this will be the last year he publishes the NSD study descriptions. The most promising of those new directions can be found in a study of potential economic benefits from various media. A good example of this effort can be found in a recent article by Tom Cobb (1997) in "ECTR&D" (vol. 45, no. 4). There are benefits to be gained from different media. The benefits are economic. If media researchers and practitioners would only switch their concerns to the economics of instruction, we would discover all manner of important cost contributions from media.

———

Richard E. Clark
University of Southern California
Los Angeles, California

intro-
duction

No Significant Difference
Thomas L. Russell
North Carolina State University
Raleigh, North Carolina

More than ten years ago I decided to identify studies that would "document" the "fact" that technology improved instruction. I sought comparative studies from all the usual sources plus inquiring of colleagues, reading innumerable articles, and following up on references. I soon discovered that there were very few comparative studies that, in fact, found that there was any measurable benefit to learning attributable to technology, and many of these were offset by studies indicating that technology-based instruction was less educationally effective. A startling finding was that there were/are an enormous number of studies — by far the vast majority of comparative ones — that showed no significant difference, at least in strategic parts of the conclusions. I wondered why "we" are seemingly so unaware of these studies or if they are being ignored because the existence of them in such large numbers tends to negate our claims of "improving" instruction through technology. I started collecting these no significant difference works and providing this information to all who showed an interest. I have also challenged anyone to create a comparable listing of comparative studies showing that technology was noticeably beneficial. No one I know of has accepted that challenge; I feel certain that some have tried and realized the futility of the search. I did not use any scientific sampling method but instead listed every study found that showed no significant difference. For those who criticize me for not listing favorable studies, I again issue the above-mentioned challenge. The point remains that such studies are practically nonexistent and the very few that do exist are offset by a like number which show negative results for the technology-based instruction. The good news is that these no significant difference studies provide substantial evidence that technology does not denigrate instruction. This fact opens doors to employing technologies to increase efficiencies, circumvent obstacles, bridge distances, and the like. It also allows us to employ cheaper and simpler technologies with assurance that outcomes will be comparable with the more sophisticated and expensive ones as well as conventional teaching/learning methods.

When I cite the overwhelming number of no significant difference findings, I generally leave it to the readers to interpret what those studies mean to them. Some become frustrated and immediately search the listings for any flawed studies because they are convinced that the technologies somehow improve learning. These studies tell me that there is nothing inherent in the technologies that elicits improvements in learning. Having said that, let me reassure you that differences in outcomes can be made more positive by adapting the content to the technology. That is, in going through the process of redesigning a course to adapt the content to the technology, it can be improved. The mere process is where the difference lies.

Tom Russell

Clark (1994) states that:

> ...if learning occurs as a result of exposure to any media, the learning is caused by the instructional method embedded in the media presentation. Method is the inclusion of one of a number of possible representations of a cognitive process or strategy that is necessary for learning but which students cannot or will not provide for themselves. (p. 26)

> ..if different media or attributes yield similar learning gains and facilitate achievement of necessary performance criteria, then in a design science or an instructional technology, we must always choose the less expensive way to achieve a learning goal. I must also form out theories around the underlying structural features of the shared properties of the interchangeable variables and not base theory on the irrelevant surface features. (p. 22)

In an article, "Soft Technologies: Instructional and Informational Design Research," in Jonassen (1996), Robert D. Tennyson states:

> I agree with Clark and believe that our instructional technology research needs to focus more on processes and less on media. One need only attend conferences fairly regularly to see that our field runs through fads or favorite media in cycles. At the time of this writing, hypermedia and multimedia are popular applications and foci of research. Yet both are simply kinds of media used to support instructional methods. (p. 685)

Some consider these findings encouraging as they can now apply technology with full assurance that they will not likely do harm to the instruction — it will be as good at the other end as it is at the origination site. They are now "free" to proceed with confidence that they will likely do as well as they do in the classroom or with other technologies and can capitalize on the uniquenesses of the technology to, for example, reach new constituencies, save funds, and/or reach some of their students (even those in the classroom) whose learning styles are better suited to the new technology as opposed to a previous one or the classroom. In the paper introducing the first version of this compilation in 1992 (included in the following section) I wrote:

> No matter how it is produced, how it is delivered, whether or not it is interactive, low-tech, or high-tech students learn equally well with each technology and learn as well as their on-campus, face-to-face counterparts.

At that time, I naively thought that notice would be taken of the then-136 *No Significant Difference* listings as well as that bold statement. I was hopeful that the paper would make an impact and/or create controversy, especially since many were promising to improve learning through technology and most were sure that instruction delivered by technology was inferior. While the recognition the paper received — and continues to receive — is gratifying as well as controversial, it nonetheless seems that it has made far less difference than had been hoped. Now, more than six years later, with the number of citations almost tripled, one continues to hear of the goal of instructional improvement through technology, and that technology-based instruction is at a lower quality than the traditional classroom. Pittman (1997) states:

> For those charged with creating programs, the good news is that a wealth of evidence supports the position that distance education programs match conventional, on-campus, face-to-face courses in both rigor and quality of outcomes. The bad news is that in spite of the large number of these studies that are performed and presented, nobody ever seems to notice them. Students, administrators, and faculty continue to act as if they were the first to whom the question of comparative outcomes had ever occurred. (p. 42)

The majority of practitioners still insist on costly, cumbersome, and access-limiting accouterments such as synchronous interactivity, and allude to the common nonsense of the profession. Worst of all is the incessant ignoring and/or outright dismissal of comparative research, seemingly because it constantly produces results counter to the wishes of the "researcher." Instead there are such comments as, "the right questions haven't been asked," "the studies are flawed," and, "there is too little research in this area." The latest technologies to enter the arena are those that are computer based. Will they break the No Significant Difference pattern? It was hoped so, but this book includes more than 40 studies on various aspects of this "new" computer-based instruction that have elicited no significant difference outcomes. In an article, "Cooperation and the Use of Technology," in Jonassen (1996) David W. Johnson and Roger T. Johnson pose two questions with answers:

> Does technology effect achievement or is it merely a means of delivering instruction? In a review of research Clark (1983) concluded that technology is merely a means of delivering instruction. Our results support this conclusion. (p. 1037)

Is the effectiveness of a message separate from the medium? Generally, the research on cognitive development indicates that the same information, presented in other formats (especially nonsocial formats) is only marginally effective in promoting genuine cognitive development (Murray, 1983; Johnson & Johnson, 1989). (p. 1038)

I am most thankful to those who have taken the time to contact me and share with me their appreciation for my efforts. It has been a fascinating and rewarding journey. The interest this work has identified has been both overwhelming and gratifying. I have responded to hundreds of world-wide requests for hard copies and there have been more than 25,000 hits, in just the last six months, on the home page at the University of New Brunswick. To those who have benefitted from electronic or print versions of the material, knowing of those gains has been satisfying. To those who seek and find the "weaknesses" in my presentation, I ask that you disregard those weaknesses to see the big picture. If that is the case, I shall be gratified if I have made a difference, albeit insignificant.

———

A site, http://tenb.mta.ca/phenom/, has been established at the University of New Brunswick to provide current updates (citations) for readers to submit "no significant difference" and "significant difference" entries for permanent posting.

original article

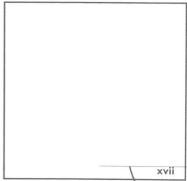

The following is a letter from Carol A. Twigg in the NLII Viewpoint—Educational National Learning Infrastructure Initiative and is reprinted by permission of EDUCOM (now EDUCAUSE). The article referred to originally appeared in the October 1992 issue of *Research in Distance Education* published by Athabasca University. While the article was focused on television-based technologies, the conclusions are equally applicable to all technologies. An ever-increasing number of these "no significant difference" results are now being realized by the newest computer-based technologies, and the conclusions stated therein seem to be equally attributable to these "cutting edge" technologies in spite of the growing chorus of claims to the contrary. Many thanks to Carol Twigg for her insightful comments and for consenting to their reproduction in this book.

Who hasn't participated in a discussion about learning and information technology without hearing someone say "We need research" or "We need to prove . . . No one knows." A recent example of this phenomenon occurred on a listserve whose primary purpose sometimes appears to be to question every possible advance in using technology: "Before we commit ourselves to 'the virtual classroom' or even the 'virtual university,' I would like to see solid empirical research that shows that undergraduates will learn how to think critically, interact rationally, and develop the cognitive and ethical perspectives that they acquire in a good residential program." In this 1992 article, Tom Russell asks, "Does anyone ever really read research reports?" It's clear the person who made the foregoing statement doesn't. I must admit I don't. But with Tom keeping tabs on the research on instructional media, I don't have to.

Tom Russell is the authority on the "no significant difference" phenomenon. He has created a compendium of more than 200 relevant citations and excerpts illustrating this phenomenon. His compendium is available on the Web (http://teleeducation.nb.ca/phenom/), selections from which are included here. Confirming Richard Clark's meta-analysis of research findings on learning and media, which was included in the first *NLII Viewpoint*, Tom states emphatically, "The fact is that the findings of comparative studies are absolutely conclusive; one can bank on them. No matter how it is produced, how it is delivered, whether or not it is interactive, low-tech or high-tech, students learn equally well with each technology and learn as well as their on-campus, face-to-face counterparts even though students would rather be on campus with the instructor if that were a real choice."

Comparative studies have shown that people learn as well from traditional print-based correspondence courses as they do from the most slickly produced and/or interactive telecourses. Tom's article that accompanies the excerpts focuses on instructional television to illustrate the distinction between effective learning and the use of various kinds of technologies. In it, he rightly debunks those who insist on high-cost, slick-production, broadcast-quality interactive television when research has shown that low-cost video systems are equally effective. Tom's emphasis is on providing effective access for students at the lowest possible cost. As he says, "While some traveling to Europe might agree that the best way to go would be on the Concorde, being denied the lower cost options that would still get one there would be unthinkable." This article is characteristic of Tom Russell's work: he is eminently rational in his approach (the antithesis of "don't confuse me with the facts!"), and his attention stays fixed where it should be—on effective learning rather than on technology.

Carol A. Twigg

Reprinted with permission from *Research in Distance Education*, October 1992

Television's Indelible Impact on Distance Education: What We Should Have Learned from Comparative Research by Thomas L. Russell

Does anyone ever really read research reports on instructional television? It does not seem so, unless it is to look for an occasional tidbit that might be construed as proof to support what was intended to be done all along. Another reason for reading these reports might be to condemn the now totally predictable "no significant difference" results, and declare that too many individuals read these documents looking for the question that fits the answer already "known"—not unlike Johnny Carson's Carnac.

There has been so much research on instructional television in all of its manifestations—slickly produced, candid classroom, telecourses, interactive, ITFS, videotape, satellite—at all levels and all over the United States that it seems incredible that there is such a high level of ignorance (or is it denial?) of the results. Of course, there are a few contradictions, but there can be a high degree of confidence in drawing firm conclusions from voluminous studies. The fact is that the findings of comparative studies are absolutely conclusive; one can bank on them. No matter how it is produced, how it is delivered, whether or not it is interactive, low tech or high tech, students learn equally well with each technology and learn as well as their on-campus, face-to-face counterparts even though students would rather be on campus with the instructor if that were a real choice.

It is also true that many faculty are reluctant to participate on a voluntary basis and will be intimidated by the technology. Often that intimidation will manifest itself in an "uncomfortable" performance for those who do participate. Further, it is abundantly clear that faculty and administration tend to feel that the quality of the instruction for the distance student is inferior to that given to the on-campus, face-to-face student.

If one were to accept the preceding premises and design a new television-based delivery system based on these facts, should it look like any of the current high-tech, high-profile, fiber optic, satellite, broadcast-quality, interactive, highly vaunted system? Absolutely not—unless ignoring what should have been learned from comparative studies and experience continues. High-tech systems are vastly more expensive than low-tech ones. Despite the fact that all systems are equally effective, why is it we continue to elect the most costly, cumbersome, teacher-unfriendly technologies? There is at least one system in existence that was established based on previous knowledge (research) available. This system, the VideoClass System, proves that one can learn from research, and can solve specific problems when they are isolated and simplified.

The VideoClass System, an offshoot/improvement of the candid classroom, is alive and well at North Carolina State University. Since research has proven that any delivery system, regardless of (low) cost, has virtually identical (learning) results, the candid classroom approach was significantly modified. Faculty reluctance has been overcome through a totally new, faculty-dominated, nonintimidating, minimally yet significantly changed candid classroom facility along with operational procedures.

Possibly there are other equally successful programs, but, unlike the VideoClass System, they are not likely to garner any real attention since they lack the sex appeal of super-high-tech, cutting-edge systems. Perhaps it is unfair to criticize these very expensive, newsworthy systems as they are, after all, equally effective.

Almost 10 years ago the Review of Educational REsearch stated and documented, "The best current evidence is that media are mere vehicles that deliver instruction but do not influence achievement any more than the truck that delivers our groceries causes changes in nutrition. . . only the content of the vehicle can influence achievement (Clark, 1983; p.445) Yet, our high-tech propensities seem to compel us to embrace the most visible (sophisticated) technologies, which also exacerbated expense, scheduling difficulties, and other limiting factors. It is time for educators to again take control—take it from the gadgeteers and preachers of erroneous common nonsense. It is time to objectively evaluate what research has taught, and to cast off the stifling, disproved yet pervasive myths of broadcasters and technologists who have imposed unnecessary, self-serving constraints.

It would be naive to think that this one article would have any real impact regarding the onrush to employ all available technology, regardless of cost and relative effectiveness, to reach distant learners. After all everyone knows high-tech, interactive, broadcast quality television teaches better. . . everyone may "know" except those who know about the research. There is no quarrel with the desirability of broadcast quality, and interactivity, but there is an argument against denying potential students who could be taught with lower-cost, equally effective, more flexible options on the grounds that the best way to go would be on the Concorde being denied the lower cost options that would still get one there would be unthinkable. Imagine what might be done for mankind if self-interested, high-tech dreams could be dispensed with, and action taken with equal enthusiasm based on the absolute knowledge available. What might happen if insisting on the disproved broadcast-quality, interactive, commercial-type production, high-tech (satellite/fiber) course development ceased?

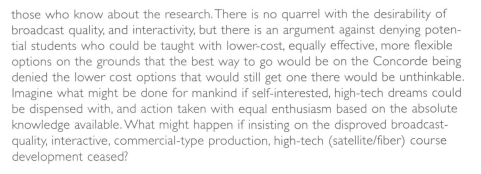

xx

In place of this common nonsense try substituting research-based uncommon sense—good classroom teaching (there are still good teachers, and they can be kept that way if they have not been spoiled with common nonsense) and an appropriately designed and operated low-tech system. Heeding research and carefully downsizing the technology it is possible to:

1. lower cost of instructional television by a factor of 100, perhaps 1000

2. increase course offerings by a comparable number

3. attract, by a similar factor, more volunteer instructors

4. fulfill many more educational needs of the community

5. serve very small as well as large publics

6. respond very quickly with finished, readily updated distance instruction

7. under certain conditions where revenues (tuition) can be generated, provide self-supporting, even profitable, operations.

All this and more could be achieved with research-based confidence; students will learn as well in both the classroom or at a distant site.

It is known, unequivocally, what makes the defendable sense and that which is nonsense. Unfortunately, it seems to have been turned around, and the headlong rush is toward high-tech, interactive systems based entirely on common nonsense while the uncommon sense of low-tech, e.g. the VideoClass System, is completely overlooked.

At one time accountability was an education buzzword. Comparative studies also show that people learn as well from traditional, print-based correspondence courses as they do from the most slickly produced and/or interactive telecourses. Where is the accountability with the knowledge that today's high-tech systems are no more effective than low-tech alternatives such as correspondence courses or the VideoClass System?

Is it still necessary to have conventional television producers and systems? Yes, but their role needs to be that of producers of programming that is useful within the classroom and, therefore, useful in low-tech video systems. At the same time, a new breed of "producer" would not be overly interested in technology but in how to employ the components of the media in the lease expensive, demonstratively (research-based) most effective manner to meet the needs of the students.

It should not be a surprise, when the television producer/specialist and other technology-oriented staff are asked for their reaction to these research findings, that they strongly reject all these findings and insist these voluminous comparative studies are erroneous, or at least, not applicable in their situation. This problem is exacerbated by the propensity on the part of the administration and faculty to be predisposed to believe in the necessity for slick production, broadcast quality, and interactivity.

It is folly to disagree with those who say that it it time to stop asking questions about instructional television's effectiveness. It works. Research tells us that it does not improve learning, but it can surely do as well. Here are a few questions researchers should consider:

1. Why do students learn equally well via means such as classroom, correspondence, VideoClass Systems, PBS, audiotape, other?

2. Why are empirical research results ignored to the detriment of constituencies?

3. Why do professional educators embrace high-cost technologies when low-cost technologies work as well?

4. How can administration and faculty—despite research results—perceive that instructional television, especially without interaction, is inferior?

5. Why does interactivity achieve no better results in learning when individual students and teachers believe that it does?

6. How can technology-based distance student drop-out rates be improved?

If one day the lessons of the existing voluminous research were to be accepted, the promise to improve education with the instructional technology would cease, and the proven fact that it can be delivered with the same quality as classroom instruction would be cause for rejoicing. When the day comes that increased sophistication of technologies is shown conclusively to improve learning, then and only then should the promise be restated.

acknow-ledge-ments

As might be expected, a publication of this magnitude required the assistance of many without whom it would not have been completed. A thank you is due to Richard Clark for his insightful foreword and his willingness to lend his endorsement and prestige to the effort. Rory McGreal from the University of New Brunswick offered his services and made the content of previous versions of this book available world wide on his university's home page. He has also committed to maintain the site to update this book.

A thank you to all who contributed
entries, especially to Von Pittman from the
University of Missouri-Columbia.
A special thank you goes to Ella Hannan
for belief in your son. My greatest appreciation is for the editorial and inspirational
support from Jane D. Russell, my beloved
wife, who indeed made a significant difference in my work and my life.

Thomas L. Russell
North Carolina State University
Raleigh North Carolina   U.S.A.
1999

chrono-
logical
listing
of entrie

"...**no differences** in test scores of college classroom and correspondence study students enrolled in the same subjects."

"[Results of this study were very similar to Crump 1928 and showed]...**no differences** in test scores of college classroom and correspondence study students enrolled in the same subjects..."

"One group saw the speaker, and the other group heard him from another room [on a loud speaker]. The direct group performed better, but later tests showed that the means were **not significantly different**."

"In all but two comparisons, correspondence study students performed **as well as or better than** their classroom counterparts and in the two cases which were \the exception the differences were not significant."

"...a comparison in tests taken after a week showed **little difference** in methods employed."

"The results, also using the test, showed that phonographic recordings **failed to show any superior effectiveness** in teaching the 'informational' aspects of the lesson."

1928

Crump, R. E.
Correspondence and Class Extension Work in Oklahoma
Doctoral Dissertation, Teachers College
Columbia University; New York, NY

1936

Sorenson, H.
Comparative Abilities of Extension and Non-Extension Students
Twenty-third Annual Meeting
Association of Urban Universities, 54-60

1937

Loder, J. E.
A Study of Aural Learning With and Without the Speaker Present
Journal of Experimental Education 6, 49-60

1940

Hanna, L. N.
Achievement of High School Students in Supervised Correspondence Study
Master's Thesis
University of Nebraska; Lincoln, NE

1943

Rulon, P. V.
A Comparison of Phonographic Recordings with Printed Material in Terms of Knowledge
The Harvard Educational Review 8, 63-76

1943

Rulon, P. V.
A Comparison of Phonographic Recordings with Printed Material in Terms of Knowledge Gained Through Their Use as a Teaching Unit
The Harvard Educational Review 8, 163-75

"showed **no significant differences** between the groups in terms of motivation to use supplementary reading material."

"The results of the study yielded **no significant difference** between the reading and listening groups. The most significant finding . . . the radio group did equally well as compared to the standard reading group . . . [also] reviewed several research studies that were designed to compare the effectiveness of instructional radio with traditional methods . . . **no significant difference** in achievement resulted from the majority of reviewed."

"[Results of this study were very similar to Hanna 1940 and showed . . .] in all but two comparisons, correspondence study students performed as well as or better than their classroom counterparts and in the two cases which were the exception, **the differences were not significant**."

"[Results of this study were very similar to Hannah 1940 and Meierhenry 1946 and showed . . .] in all by two comparisons, correspondence study students performed as well as or better than their classroom counterparts and in the two cases which were the exception, **the differences were not significant**."

1943

Rulon, P. V.
A Comparison of Phonographic Recordings with Printed Motivation to Further Study
The Harvard Educational Review 8, 246-55

1945

Woelfel, N. and Tyler, I. K.
Radio and the School
World Book Tarrytown-on-Hudson New York

1946

Meierhenry, W. C.
A Vocational Education Program for the Small High School Utilized Supervised Correspondence Study and Work Experience
Doctoral Dissertation
University of Nebraska; Lincoln, NE

1949

Childs, G. B.
A Comparison of Supervised Correspondence Study Pupils and Classroom Pupils in Achievement in School Subjects
Doctoral Dissertation
University of Nebraska; Lincoln, NE

"...the difference in scores between the two groups **was significantly less** when standardized tests were used as measures of achievement."

1949

Scott, G.
A Study of the Contribution of Motion Pictures to the Educational Achievement in Nebraska High Schools
University of Nebraska; Lincoln, NE

"...compared ninth-grade biology students taught by: (1) sound films, (2) sound films plus study guides, and (3) standard lecture demonstration classroom instruction. **No significant differences** were found across all groups on either immediate or three-month-delayed achievement testing..."

1950

VanderMeer, A. W.
Relative Effectiveness of Instruction of Films Exclusively, Films Plus Study Guides, and Standard Lecture Methods
(technical report No. SDC 269-7-13)
Port Washington
U.S. Naval Training Devices Center;
New York, NY

"The author concludes that open-circuit TV is **an effective means** of reaching college credit students in their homes."

1952

Stromberg, E. L.
College for Television Home Study
American Psychologist 7, 507-509

"The results showed that there were **no significant differences** on the cooperative measures."

1953

Brushwood, J. and Polmantier, P.
The Effectiveness of the Audio-Laboratory in Elementary Modern Language Courses
University of Missouri; Columbia, MO

"TV is an **equally effective**, compared to face-to-face, means of instruction..."

1954

Anderson, G. R. & VanderMeer, A. W.
A Comparative Study of the Effectiveness of Lessons on the Slide Rule Presented via Television and in Person
Mathematics Teacher 47, 323-327

"In five of 17 tests given, the TV group scored significantly higher. In the remaining 12 tests **no significant differences** were found."

1954

Kanner, J. H., Runyon, R. P., & Desiderato, O.
Television in Army Training: Evaluation of Television in Army Basic Training
George Washington University;
Washington, D.C.

"Television instruction was found to be **as effective** as classroom instruction in teaching facts...No significant differences were found between the TV-only and TV-plus-practice groups..."

1954

Shimberg, B.
Effectiveness of Television in Teaching *Home Nursing Educational Testing Service*
Research Bulletin, RB-54-19

1955

Carpenter, C. R. & Greenhill, L. P.
An Investigation of Closed-Circuit Television for Teaching University Courses
Instructional Television Research
Project Number One
Pennsylvania State University; University Park, PA

"The difference between the effectiveness of televised instruction versus conventional instruction was **not statistically significant**..."

1955

Fotos, J. T.
The Purdue Laboratory Method in Teaching Beginning Classes
Modern Language Journal 39, 141-43

"Whether there was **a significant difference cannot be ascertained**."

1955

Frank, J. H.
An Evaluation of Closed Circuit Television for Interceptor Pilot Training
Dissertation Abstracts 15, 2060-2061

"...**no significant differences** in test scores..."

1956

Carpenter, C. R. & Greenhill, L. P.
Instructional Film Reports, Vol. 2
(Technical Report No. 269-7-61)
Port Washington
NY: Special Devices Center, U. S. Navy

"The findings of these studies...indicated **no significant differences**..."

1956

Dowell, E. C.
An Experiment in Training by Television
Audio-Visual Communication Review
"It was concluded that the presentation methods were equally effective."

"It was conducted that the presentation methods were **equally effective**."

"...the effects of television as a variable operating in a field of perhaps hundreds of other potential variables is of minor significance. Therefore, **no significant differences** in results are to be expected."

"TV instruction was **as effective as** face-to-face instruction in teaching both algebra & physics."

"...**no significant differences** in achievement test scores between ITV and face-to-face students...no significant differences in achievement test scores between high ability ITV students and high-ability face-to-face students... Similar results were obtained for low ability students."

"...radio students performed at least **equally as well as** live audiences."

"...**no significant differences** in the final grades of ITV and face-to-face students..."

"Analysis of variance on television, lecture, and discussion groups achievement scores indicated **no significant differences** among groups on either of two achievement tests."

1956

Kumata, H.
An Inventory of Instructional Television Research
University of Michigan; Ann Arbor, MI

1956

Lund, K. W., Englehart, M. D., Nee, M. M.
Teaching Algebra & Physics by Means of TV
Chicago School Board Journal 38, 1-9

1956

Macomber, F. G., et al.
Experimental Study in Instructional Procedures
Miami University; Oxford, OH
Oct. 1, 1956

1956

NHK Radio-Television Cultural Research Institute
The Listening Effect of Radio English Classroom
Tokyo, Japan

1956

Pollock, T. C., et al.
Closed-circuit Television as a Medium of Instruction 1955-56
New York University; New York, NY

1956

Stuit, D. B., et al.
An Experiment in Teaching
Iowa Closed-circuit Television Teaching Experiment: Summary Report
State University of Iowa, Iowa City, IA

1957

Becker, S. L., Dunlap, R., & Gerber, J. C.
A Comparison of Three Methods of Teaching Modern Literature
The State University of Iowa, Iowa City, IA

"...part of a class discussed in the studio with the instructor while the rest of the class watched. There were **no differences** in the final performances..."

1957

Benschoter, R. P. & Charles, Don C.
Retention of Classroom & Television Learning
Journal of Applied Psychology 41, 253-256

"Students taught by TV retained their material over 3 years **as well as** students taught by face-to-face methods of instruction."

1957

Davis, R., Johnson, C., Dietrich, J.
Closed-Circuit Television Experimentation on Campus (unpublished)
Michigan State University; East Lansing, MI

"...**no statistically significant difference** between the two groups, over two successive quarters using different methods of analysis...How well do the students like courses taught via closed-circuit TV? An analysis of variance revealed no difference among the TV and non-TV groups."

1957

Himmler, M. L.
An Analysis & Evaluation of a Television Demonstration of the Teaching of Fifth-Grade Reading, Arithmetic, & French
Dissertation Abstracts 17, 2467

"...**no significant differences** in scores of pupils in the ITV and non-ITV groups on the standardized tests."

1957

Lofthouse, Y. M. S.
An Experiment with Closed-Circuit Television Instruction in Teacher Education
Dissertation Abstracts 17, 1513

"...**no significant differences** in students' attitudes toward the course, whether taught on ITV or by face-to-face methods..."

1957

Macomber, F. G., et al.
Experimental Study in Instructional Procedures
Miami University; Oxford, OH

"...**no significant differences** between scores of students in face-to-face or ITV classes when students were divided by ability levels."

"...compared instruction by kinescope, correspondence study, and classroom procedures in a course in child development and found **no advantage** for any one procedure."

1957

Parsons, T. S.
A Comparison of Instruction by Kinescope, Correspondence Study and Customary Classroom Procedures
Journal of Educational Psychology, 48: 27-40

"There were **no differences** in learning."

1958

Audio-Visual Communications Review 6, 77-78
Closed-circuit Television Instruction
Purdue University; West Lafayette, IN

"...studies of the comparative effectiveness of conventional and televised instruction, even though carefully designed to control variables...yielded **non-significant differences** in student's achievement scores."

1958

Carpenter, C. R. & Greenhill, L. P.
An Investigation of Closed Circuit Television for Teaching University Courses
Instructional Television Research,
Report no.2
Pennsylvania State University; University Park, PA

"Analysis of variance indicated **no significant differences** in achievement scores..."

1958

Champa, V. A.
Television: Its Effectiveness in Ninth-Grade Science Teaching
Audio-Visual Communications Review 6, 100-203

"Gains in knowledge were found in both groups, and there was **no significant difference** in the gain between the two classes."

1958

Cutler, R. L., McKeachie, W. J. & McNeil, E. B.
Teaching Psychology by Telephone
The American Psychologist 13(9), 551-52

"...found **no significant difference** in attitude or cognitive retention between a group viewing a single-image presentation and a group viewing a multi-image presentation."

1958

Didcoct, D. H.
Comparison of the Cognitive & Affective Responses of College Students to Single-Image and Multi-Image Audio-Visual Presentations
Unpublished doctoral dissertation
Cornell University; Ithica, NY

8

"...**no significant differences** in EPPS profiles...no significant differences among any of the three presentation groups...no significant differences among presentation methods..."

"...**no significant differences** between experimental groups and control groups..."

"**No indication** was found that intensive television sessions are more detrimental to classroom learning than face-to-face instruction."

"...**no significant differences** in achievement scores of students in the studio, in TV classrooms, and in face-to-face classes."

"...**no significant differences** in final test scores between the two groups."

"...focused strongly on comparative research designs and similarly resulted in **no significant differences.**"

1958

Dreher, R. E. & Walcott, H. B. *An Experimental Study of College Instruction Using Broadcast Television* San Francisco State College, San Francisco, CA

1958

Dyer-Bennett, J., Fuller, W. R., Seiberg, W. F. & Shanks, M. E. *Teaching Calculus by Closed-circuit Television* American Mathematical Monthly 63

1958

Kanner, J. H. et al. *Television in Army Training* Audio-Visual Communication Review 6, 255-291

1958

Los Angeles City School Districts *An Evaluation of Closed-circuit Television for Teaching Junior College Courses* Audio-Visual Communications Review 6, 237

1958

Meierhenry, W. C. *A Study of Teaching by Television Under Two Conditions* University of Nebraska; Lincoln, NE

1958

Niven, H. F. *Instructional Television as a Medium of Teaching in Higher Education* Unpublished doctoral dissertation The Ohio State University; Columbus, OH

"Students appreciated the reacher's preparation, the visuals, and the ability of television to direct attention. There were **no differences** in learning."

1958

Purdue University
Closed Circuit Television Instruction
Audio-Visual Communication Review 6, 77-78

"Students in massed groups, taught by television, appear to **learn as much** as students taught in classes, large or small, by conventional methods."

1958

Siepmann, C. A.
TV and Our School Crisis
Doff, Mead and Co.

1958

Westover, F. L., et al.
Report Evaluation the Results of Teaching Accounting I by Means of Closed-Circuit Television Presentation
University of Alabama; Tuscaloosa, AL

"Analysis of variance conducted between experimental and control groups on final examination scores and on average course scores indicated **no significant differences** between groups...**no significant differences** between groups in the number of dropouts...ITV and face-to-face students tended to make about the same grades and to do as well (or as poorly)..."

"...a majority of students **learned as much**, or more, than if they had been taught face-to-face."

1958

Wetter, A. H. & Gable, M.
Report of the National Experiment of Television Teaching in Large Classes, 1957-58
Philadelphia Public Schools

1959

Closed Circuit Television: Teaching in Washington County
The Board of Education
Hagerstown, PA

"...resulted in **no significant differences.** Few studies reported findings entirely supportive of television, and conversely few found television to be less effective than conventional classroom instruction."

"...**no significant difference** between groups on the final examination...**no significant difference** between groups on the course content test gains...**no significant difference** in the test performance..."

1959

Driscoll, J. P.
Can TV Improve College Teaching?
NAEB Journal 18

"On the final examination there was **no difference** in achievement between the students in the television classes and those in the regular classes...the average total score for the semester also revealed **no difference** in achievement between the classes taught by the two methods. It is clear, however, that in many college courses students can be expected to do equally well in examinations whether they have been taught by a teacher in a regular classroom or by the same teacher over television. When the final scores were adjusted to compensate for the initial inequality, it was found that there was **no difference** among students..."

SUMMARY OF FINDINGS AT PENN STATE
Comparative Effectiveness

1. In 29 out of 32 controlled comparisons in seven different courses, there were **no significant differences** in achievement between students taught via closed circuit television and those taught in the conventional manner.

2. In three different courses, there were **no significant differences** between scores on course-related aptitude tests taken by students taught via TV and those taught by the same teachers in the conventional way.

3. **No significant differences** in students' achievements were found when proctors of varying status were used to supervise classroom groups of students in televised classes.

Ford Foundation: Teaching by Television
Summary
Fund for the Advancement of Education

chronological listing of entries

4. **No significant differences** in student achievement were found in comparisons of classes of various sizes taught via television.

5. Several methods of providing for teacher-student interactions were studied in different courses. These included the use of questions and answers over an intercommunication system between the TV classrooms and originating room, and the rotation of students through the TV originating room. **Neither** of these **methods produced measurable increments** in learning, but the students strongly favored the use of the intercommunication system."

Ford Foundation: Teaching by Television Summary, (continued)

"...**no significant differences** in final examination scores between ITV and face-to-face students..."

1959

Gordon, O. M., Nordquist, E. C., & Engar, K. M.
Teaching the Use of the Slide Rule via Television
University of Utah; Salt Lake City, UT

"...focused strongly on comparative research designs and similarly resulted in **no significant differences**."

1959

Hagerstown Board of Education
Closed Circuit Television: Teaching in Washington County 1958-68

"...included hundreds of studies covering many content areas and many different age groups...resulted in **no significant differences**."

1959

Holmes, P. D.
Television Research in the Teaching-Learning Process
Division of Broadcasting
Wayne State University; Detroit, MI

"...there was **no statistically signifi-cant difference** between TV and face-to-face taught groups."

Irwin, J. V. & Aronson, A. E.
Television Teaching: Conventional Lecture versus Highly Visualized Film Presentations
University of Wisconsin; Madison, WI

"There was **no significant difference** between methods of instruction..."

Jacobs, J. N. & Bollenbacher, J. K.
An Experimental Study of the Effectiveness of Television versus Classroom Instruction in Sixth Grade Science in the Cincinnati Public Schools 1956-57
Journal of Educational Research 52, 184-189

"...**no consistent difference**s between the scores of the experimental and control groups. Aptitude level was more important than the instructional medium in determining test performance."

Kanner, J. H., Katz, S. & Goldsmith, P. B.
Evaluation of "Intensive" Television for Teaching Basic Electricity
Audio-Visual Communications Review 7, 307-308

"...**no significant differences** in achievement scores of students taking the course by ITV and those who had taken it face-to-face."

King. C. E. *A Comparative Study of the Effectiveness of Teaching a Course in Remedial Mathematics to College Students by Television & by the Conventional Method* Dissertation Abstracts 20, 2177

"Pupils in the TV classes **learned as much** subject matter as children in the control (face-to-face) classes."

Pflieger, E. F.
Detroit TV Teaching Project: Report for the Year 1957-58
Detroit Public Schools

"...there were **no significant differences** in spelling achievement among any of the three groups."

Phillips, J. A.
A Study Designed to Determine the Spelling Learning Which May be Attributed to Specific Series of Spelling Lessons Presented by Television
Dissertation Abstracts 20, 2182-2183

13

"Children **learn as much**, and as fast by television, as under normal conditions...students generally prefer to receive instruction live rather than over instructional television, but they apparently do not learn more."

"...**no significant differences** between radio high-medium-, and low-ability groups and ITV high-medium-, and low-ability groups on delayed recall scores."

"...compared favorably with classroom students."

"...**no significant differences** between the scores of ITV and face-to-face pupils..."

"...**no significant difference** in learning between the groups taught by an instructor with feedback and those taught by an instructor without feedback. Feedback, as provided in this study, **does not appear to have a significant effect on communication**."

"Children in larger than normal sized classes **learned as much** from televised instruction as those in conventional sized classrooms...students tended to learn as much from television teaching as from face-to-face teaching."

1959

Swartout, S. G.
Report on Findings in Educational Television
NEA Department of Audio Visual Instruction

1959

Westley, B. H. & Barrow, L. C.
Exploring the News: A Comparative Study of the Teaching Effectiveness of Radio & Television
University of Wisconsin; Madison, WI

1960

Almstead, F. E. & Graf, R. W.
Talkback: The Missing Ingredient
State Department of Education
New York

1960

Jacobs, J. N. & Bollenbacher, J. K.
Teaching Ninth Grade Biology by Television
Audio-Visual Communication Review 8, 176-191

1960

Johnson, F. C.
Feedback in Instructional Television Journal of Communication 10, 140-146

1960

Johnson, G. N. & Harty, F.
The Norfolk City Experiment in Instructional Television: The Big Picture
September 1957-June 1960
Educational Television Project
Norfolk City Public Schools

"...**no significant differences** between groups in the number of color or noncolor test items answered correctly."

1960

Kanner, J. H. & Rosenstein, A. J.
Television in Army Training:
Color vs. Black & White
Audio-Visual Communication Review 8,
243-252

1960

The Nebraska Experimental Program in the
Use of Television & Correspondence Study
University of Nebraska; Lincoln, NE

"Achievement in algebra, literature, and general mathematics was **about the same** for the face-to-face and television groups."

1960

Reid, J. C.
An Experimental Study of a Comparison of
Content Learned, Attitude Toward Subject
Matters, and Attitude Toward Instructional
Television of Students in a Public Speaking
Course Presented by Television and Face-to-
Face Methods
University of Missouri; Columbia, MO

"...**no significant differences** between the two sections in mean scores on either the mid-semester or the final subject matter test, and there were **no significant differences** between the two sections on final grades...**no significant differences** between the two sections on attitudes toward public speaking scores for any of the testings."

1960

Seibert, W. F. & Honig, J. M.
A Brief Study of Televised Laboratory
Instruction
Audio-Visual Communication Review 8,
115-123

"...**no significant differences**... only one difference in six comparisons-this in favor of the television group... An analysis of variance indicated **no significant differences** between the ITV and face-to-face groups for either the immediate or delayed post knowledge tests."

"School in American life-... **no signifi-cant differences** on final examina-tion scores... Human development-... **no significant differences** for any of the three examinations between face-to-face and ITV students... Chemistry-... **no differences** in the final examinations... Educational psy-chology- An analysis of variance on final examination scores between face-to-face and ITV students indicated **no significant differences**."

"...**no significant differences** between ITV and face-to-face groups as determined by achievement scores...**no significant differences** between the achievement scores of ITV students in homogeneously grouped classes and ITV students in heterogeneously grouped classes...**no significant differences** between gains of rural ITV students and rural face-to-face students."

"...**no significant difference** between TV and face-to-face taught general science groups...no differential effect for ability between methods of instruction...**no appreciable differ-ence** in ability to think critically between methods of instruction."

1960

Starlin, G. & Lallas, J. E.
Inter-institutional Teaching by Television in the Oregon State Systems of Higher Education
Report No. 1: 1957-59
Oregon State System of Higher Education

1960

Strevell, W. H.
High School Physics by Television
The Houston Area Project
University of Houston; Houston, TX

1960

Suchy, R. R. & Baumann, P. C.
The Milwaukee Experiment in Instructional Television: Evaluation Report
Milwaukee Public Schools

16

"Students in the television-correspondence group **did as well** as students in the control group. Experimental students whose local proctors were not certified teachers of mathematics did as well as experimental students whose local proctors were certified to teach mathematics. Both high and low ability students in the control group **did as well** as high and low ability students in the experimental group."

"...**no significant differences** attributable to eye-contact variations in attention, learning, or interest..."

"**No significant differences** were found among the three groups..."

"Despite the newness of television as a medium of instruction, despite all sorts of technical difficulties...the results clearly showed that students who received part of their instruction over television in large classes **did as well** as, and in many cases significantly better than, students who were taught by conventional methods in small classes."

1960

Wells, D. W.
The Relative Effectiveness of Teaching First Year Algebra by Television-Correspondence Study and Teaching First-Year Algebra by Conventional Methods
Dissertation Abstracts 20, 3137

1960

Westley, B. H. & Mobius, J. B.
The Effects of "Eye-contact" in Televised Instruction
University of Wisconsin; Madison, WI

1961

Abel, F. P.
Use of Closed-circuit Television in Teacher Education: Relationship to Achievement & Subject Matter Understanding
University of Minnesota; Minneapolis, MN

1961

Ford Foundation
ETV: A Ford Foundation Pictorial Report Fund for the Advancement of Education

chronological listing of entries

"...**no significant differences** between scores of any of the groups on the four experiments."

1961

Gropper, G. L. & Lumsdaine, A. A.
An Investigation of the Role of Selected Variables in Programmed TV Instruction
American Institute for Research

"...multiple-channel presentations **do not produce increases in learning** (however defined) over single-channel communication..."

1961

Hartman, F. R.
Single and Multi-Channel Communication: A Review of Research and a Proposed Model AV
Communication Review 9, 235-62

"...**no significant differences** between the scores of the experimental (N=5) or control (N=5) teachers on the program content test...**the performance** of students taught in part by television **was as good as**, or better than, that of students taught conventionally."

1961

Ivey, S. M. & DeMarco, N.
A Study of Closed-circuit Television as a Teaching Technique for Speech Improvement in the Public School System
University of Arkansas; Fayetteville, AR

"There was **no significant difference** between TV and face-to-face taught students...Television instruction is **equally effective** as face-to-face instruction..."

1961

Jacobs, J. N., Bollenbacher, J. & Keiffer, M.
Teaching Seventh-Grade Mathematics by Television to Homogeneously Grouped Below-Average Students
Mathematics Teacher 54, 551-555

"There was **no significant difference** in attitudes toward sociology for either method of instruction."

1961

Janes, R. W.
An Educational Experiment with On-campus Open-circuit Television
Journal of Educational Sociology 34, 300-308

"...**no significant differences** in content scores of students in the television or face-to-face treatments."

1961

Myers, L.
An Experimental Study of the Influence of the Experienced Teacher on Television
Syracuse University; Syracuse, NY

"Summarizing the results of a three-year national program in which 200,000 students from 800 public schools took part: "...whereas most comparisons **showed no significant differences**, 119 were significant in favor of TV-taught students, and 44 in favor of conventionally taught students." "...the effectiveness of using audio tape recorded lectures versus live lectures...**no significant difference** in student achievement..."

"...the effectiveness of using audio tape recorded lectures versus live lectures ... **no significant difference** in student achievement..."

"...**no significant differences** between mean scores for any of the fifteen lessons between the two groups...no definite trends that either black & white or color was more effective."

"Students **learn as effectively** in large classes taught by TV as in large classes taught face-to-face."

1961

Pflieger, E. F. & Kelly, F. G.
The National Program in the Use of Television in the Public Schools
The Ford Foundation/FAE

1961

Popham, W. J.
Tape Recorded Lectures in the College Classroom
AV Communications Review, 9

1961

Rosenstein, A. J. & Kanner, J. H.
Television in Army Training: Color vs. Black & White
Audio-Visual Communication Review 9, 44-49

1961

Rothchild, T. H. & Lastinger, R. L.
The Florida West Coast Project for the Utilization of Television in Large Class Teaching: First Year Report, July 1959 to June 1960
NAEB Journal 20, 1-2

chronological listing of entries

"**No significant differences** in effectiveness for either television or face-to-face lecture or observation were found using final grades as a criterion, and **no significant differences** were found between television and face-to-face lectures from scores on an examination given four months after the semester ended. It was concluded that television **was as effective** as face-to-face methods in learning and attitude changes in the elementary school methods course."

"From the 6 years of study, the authors concluded that students on all campuses **learned equally well** when taught by television from one campus. Students also **learned as well** when taught by television as when taught by face-to-face methods."

"...**no significant differences** among groups or posttest subject matter scores when adjusted for pretest subject matter scores, and no significant differences when adjusted for both pretest and IQ scores. Analysis of variance indicated **no significant differences** among groups on retention scores. Analysis of variance on students' attitude of teacher effectiveness on televised teaching indicated **no significant differences** among groups..."

1961

Rumford, H. P.
An Experiment in Teaching Elementary School Methods via Closed-circuit Television
Dissertation Abstracts 21, 2994

1961

Starlin, G. & Lallas, J. E.
Inter-institutional Teaching by Television in the Oregon State System of Higher Education Report No. 2: 1959-61
Oregon State System of Higher Education

1961

Wolgamuth, D.
A Comparative Study of Three Techniques of Student Feedback in Television Teaching: The Effectiveness of an Electrical Signal Feedback System
American University; Washington, D. C.

20

1962

"...there is **no difference** in achievement scores between the television and non-television lectures..."

Alexander, F. D.
An Experiment in Teaching Mathematics at the College Level by Closed-circuit Television
Dissertation Abstracts 22, 2805

1962

"...**no significant differences** were found between these two levels for French phoneme discrimination."

Buka, M., Freeman, M. K. & Locke, W. N.
Language Learning and Frequency Response
International Journal of American Linguistics 28, 62-79

1962

"...**no significant differences** between television and face-to-face lecture-discussion groups in changing teacher's attitudes toward the in-services program, or in changing teacher's understanding of mathematics and methods or in changing mathematics achievement and interest of pupils."

Devault, M. V., Houston, W. R. & Boyd, C. C.
Television & Consultant Services as Methods of In-service Education for Elementary School Teachers of Mathematics
The University of Texas; Austin, TX

1962

"...**no significant differences** between groups taught conventionally and by television..."

Diamond, R. M.
The Effect of Closed Circuit Resource Television upon Achievement in the Laboratory Phase of a Functional Anatomy Course: A Comprehensive Investigation of Television as a Magnification Device During Laboratory Demonstrations
Dissertation Abstracts 23, 884

1962

"...**no significant differences** in science reasoning scores..."

Dietmeier, H. J.
The Effects of the Integration of Science Teaching by Television on the Development of Scientific Reasoning in the Fifth-Grade Student
Dissertation Abstracts 22, 3517-3518

"...**no significant differences** between face-to-face and televised instruction as determined by scores on the Watson-Glaser, MAT, Spatial Relations, and on the achievement measures."

1962

Geddes, D. C.
The Use of Television in Teaching Tenth Year Mathematics: The Effectiveness of Teaching Tenth Year Mathematics by Television and a Classroom Teacher as Compared with the Traditional Method of Instruction by a Single Classroom Teacher
Dissertation Abstracts 22, 4293

"TV appears to be an **equally effective** means of instruction compared to face-to-face instruction..."

1962

Martin, H. S.
The Relative Effectiveness of Teaching Dramatic Understanding as Compared to Conventional Classroom Instruction
University of Nebraska; Lincoln, NE

"...students in TV classes **learned as much** as students in face-to-face classes."

1962

Pflieger, E. F. & Kelly, F. C.
The National Program in the Use of Television in the Public Schools
Audio-Visual Communication Review 10, 128

"Chi-square analysis revealed **no significant difference** assorted variables...both groups had increased performance on the achievement tests; there was **no significant difference** between them. There was **no significant difference** on reactions to the courses."

1962

Popham, W. J.
Tape Recorded Lectures in the College Classroom II
AV Communication Review 10, 94-101

"...**no significant differences** among scores of students in the five groups...**no significant differences** among groups on the four rating scales."

1962

Rogers, W. F.
Television Utilization in the Observation Program for Teacher Education
San Jose State College, San Jose, CA

"...the results of 393 studies were summarized. Of these, 83 showed differences in learning in favor of television, 255 reported **no significant differences**, and 55 favored direct classroom teaching...There can no longer be any doubt that students learn efficiently from instruction television. The fact has been demonstrated now in hundreds of schools, by thousands of students, in every part of the United States and in several other countries. Instruction Television is **at least as effective** as ordinary classroom instruction, when the results are measured by the usual final examinations or by standardized tests...employing the usual tests that schools use...we can say with considerable confidence that in 65 percent of a very large number of comparisons between televised and classroom teaching, there is **no significant difference**. In 21 percent, students learned significantly more, in 14 percent, they learned significantly less, from television."

"...**no significant differences** among scores on a behavioral instrument used to record performance of the student teachers in the three treatments."

"...**no significant differences** between experimental (TV) and control (non-TV) groups in science retention or science interest and attitude."

1962

Schramm, W.
*What We Know About Learning from
Instructional Television: The Next Ten Years*
Institute for Communication Research
Stanford University; Stanford, CA

1962

Schueler, H., Gold, M. J. & Mitzel, H. E.
*The Use of Television for Improving Teacher
Training and for Improving Measures of
Student-Teaching Performance*
Phase I, Improvement of Student Teaching
Hunter College of the City of New York, NY

1963

Amirian, G. T.
*The Retention by Elementary School Children
of Natural Science Material and of Science
Attitude and Interest Changes Following a
Program of Science Teaching by Television*
Dissertation Abstracts 23, 2414

"The assessments and evaluations show at least that the use of television **does not adversely affect** the quality of instruction..."

1963

Carpenter, C. R.
Research on Instructional Television
Pennsylvania State University; University Park, PA

"**No differences** were found between mean difference scores on either of the content tests, on the scores of the problem-solving test, or on the mean difference scores on attitudes..."

1963

DeViney, R. D.
An Evaluation of Closed-circuit Television Observation for Students Taking Certain Courses in Elementary Education Dissertation Abstracts 23, 3198-3199

"**No differences** were found when achievement was compared between groups receiving instructions by television and illustrated lecture, despite a televised demonstration..."

1963

Grant, T. S., et al.
Effectiveness of Television within the Dental Laboratory
University of California San Francisco Medical Center; San Francisco, CA

"...**no significant differences** between the two groups on any of the three measurements."

1963

Greenhill, P. L., Lottes, J. J. & Pagano, A.
Comparative Research on Methods & Media [Television] for Presenting Programmed Courses in Mathematics & English
Pennsylvania State University; University Park, PA

"...**no significant differences** among scores between the two groups..."

1963

Jantzen, V. W.
The Effectiveness of Television Teaching of American Government Compared with Regular Classes in Wichita High School South Dissertation Abstracts 24, 1029

"...**no differences** between experimental and control groups..."

1963

Kansas City Public Schools
Report of the Educational Television Project in Kansas City, Missouri Public Schools 1958-59, 1959-60, 1960-61
NAEB Journal 22, 1-2

"Multiple-regression techniques showed **no significant differences** between groups..."

1963

Meacham, E. A.
The Relative Effectiveness of Face-to-Face Lecture versus Instructional Television in a College Clothing Course
Dissertation Abstracts 24, 276

"...**no significant differences** in overall achievement..."

1963

Reede, A. H. & Reede, R. K.
Televising Instruction in Elementary Economics
Pennsylvania State University; University Park, PA

"...three groups, one taught by correspondence study, one by programmed instruction, and one by a combination of the two in high school algebra and English...**no significant differences** in achievement in English or algebra and **no difference** in dropout rate."

1963

Sjogren, D.
Programmed Materials in High School Correspondence Courses
University of Nebraska; Lincoln, NE

"...**no significant difference** between methods of instruction...**No significant difference** between methods of instruction was found for attitudes..."

1963

Souder, M., et al.
Study of the Effectiveness of Televised Instruction in a Physical Education Course
NAEB Journal 22, 1-2

"...**no significant differences** between the high school TV and teaching machine groups or any of the criterion measures...**no significant differences** between the college TV and face-to-face groups on any of the achievement measures."

1963

Spencer, R. E.
Comparisons of Televised with Teaching and Televised with Instructor Presentations of English Grammar
Pennsylvania State University; University Park, PA

"...10 [studies] were classified as 'interpretable'. Of these 10, all showed **no significant differences** in learning at the .05 level...**no significant difference** in learning...between televised teaching and conventional teaching."

1963

Stickell, D. W.
A Critical Review of the Methodology and Results of Research Comparing Televised and Face-to-Face Instruction
Pennsylvania State University; University Park, PA

"...**no advantage** for an audiovisual presentation over presentations via audio and visual modalities alone."

1963

VanMondfrans, A. P.
An Investigation of the Interaction Between the Level of Meaningfulness and Redundancy in the Content of the Stimulus Material and the Mode of Presentation of the Stimulus Material
Unpublished Masters Thesis
University of Utah; Salt Lake City, UT

"There were **no differences between** the groups on scores...or on achievement in the course."

1963

Walton, N. R.
A Pilot Study of Student Attitudes in a Closed-circuit Television Course by Use of Stimulated Recall
Dissertation Abstracts 24, 1082

"The differences were **not significant**, and only with music was the small difference in the direction of the radio."

1964

Constantine, M.
Radio in the Elementary School
Science Education 48, 121-32

"The **differences were not significant**..."

1964

Cook, H. R.
The Effects of Learning of Structural Drills in Spanish Broadcast via High Frequency AM Radio (NDEA Title VII Project No. 1018)
Indiana University; Bloomington, IN

"...over a ten-year period correspondence study students and internal students of New England University in New South Wales **both showed a pass rate of 74%**."

"TEMP courses are **as effective as** face-to-face teaching. Even faculty members who may have objections to television for other reasons acknowledge this."

"...no significant differences between the scores of face-to-face and TV observation groups...Scores of the two observation groups on the class were **about the same**."

"...students learning German from closed circuit television did significantly better in aural and reading comprehension than students taught by the conventional method. However, the two groups had **no differences** on written finals."

"There were **no differences** between the groups on the cooperative test...The difference between the two groups was **not significant**... there were **no differences** between the lab and nonlab groups on the vocabulary and grammar tests."

1964

Erdos, R.
Unpublished report
New England University, Australia

1964

Greene, H.
Improvement of Teaching by Television: Current Status of the Texas Educational Microwave Project
NAEB National Conference Proceedings

1964

Sykes, R. A.
The Effectiveness of Closed-circuit Television Observation and of Direct Observation of Children's Art Classes for Implementing Teachers' Training in Art Education
Dissertation Abstracts 25, 2387

1965

Gottschalk, G. H.
Closed Circuit Television in Second Semester College German
Modern Language Journal

1965

Lorge, S. W.
Comments on "Language Laboratory Research: A Critique"
Modern Language Journal 49, 369-70

"...students taught by television learned content **as well as** or better than those taught without it...judged equal in the teaching of elementary music... found the TV group of medical school students superior, but not significantly so."

"...the comprehension of the distribute practice group was **as good** or better than the comprehension demonstrated by the mass practiced group...**no** particular **method** of training or practice appears to be **any more effective** than another."

"...examined 112 studies that compared programmed instruction with conventional instruction and found that on measures of achievement 41 showed programmed instruction superior, 6 showed programmed instruction significantly worse, and 37 showed **no significant difference** between the two treatments."

"...studies preponderantly **document no significant** differences in the measured results of the two modes of instruction."

"Oregon reported students **learning as well**. The Hagerstown experiment reported that in no subject did TV fail to produce results at least as good as those achieved when classroom instruction alone was used."

1965

Razik, T. A.
What Instructional Television Research Tells Us
State University of New York at Buffalo, NY

1966

Friedman, H. L., Orr, D. & Norris, C.
Further Research on Speeded Speech as an Educational Medium—the Use of Listening Aids

1966

Hartley, J.
New Education

1966

Murphy, J. & Gross, R.
Learning by Television: The Question of Quality
Academy for Educational Development, Inc.

1966

Skornia, H. J.
What *We Know from New Media Research*
NAEB

"Of the 421 separate comparisons made ...308 showed **no significant differences**, 63 showed television instruction to be superior, and 50 found conventional instruction better. In a total of 202 comparisons of television and conventional teaching at the college level, 152 showed **no significant difference** in student performance, 22 showed television to be more effective, and 28 showed conventional teaching to be more effective."

"The findings of these studies, however, indicated **no significant differences** in most cases...studies focused on the relative effectiveness of instructional films for teaching performance skills and generally found **no significant difference**. The effects of production variables [showed] **few, if any significant differences** across groups."

"The vast majority of these studies has **revealed no significant differences** in measured performances between students who were instructed via television, and those who were taught directly."

"Pre- and post-test results showed **no significant differences** in mastery of content; student course evaluations showed **no difference** in student attitudes."

"...there is no statistical basis to conclude that TV itself **affects** learning situations or grades **positively or negatively**..."

1967

Chu, G. C. & Schramm, W.
Learning from Television
Stanford University; Stanford, CA

1967

Greenhill, L. P.
Review of Trends in Research on Instructional Television and Film
In J. C. Reid & D. W. MacLennan, eds
Research via Instructional Television and Film
U. S. Office of Education

1967

Reid, J. C. and MacLennan, D. W.
Review of Trends in Research on Instructional Television and Film
University of Missouri; St. Louis, MO

1968

Boswell, J. J., Mocker, D. W. & Hamlin, W. C.
Telelecture: An Experiment in Remote Teaching Adult Leadership

1968

Chu, G. C. & Schramm, W.
Learning from Television: What the Research Says
National Association of Educational Broadcasters

"The results from the first year indicated **no significant differences** between the teaching strategies...There were **no significant differences** detected between laboratory systems."

"Media comparison studies, regardless of media employed, tend to result in **no significant differences**..."

"There is no longer any question as to the efficacy of television in extending and improving instruction in higher education. In nearly every situation where it has been tried and carefully evaluated, results show that it permits learning **equal to** and not rarely superior to that achieved under traditional classroom practices."

"...there is no convincing evidence that multiple-channel communications **were any more effective** in producing learning than single-channel inputs."

"The overall distribution of grades for students who saw lectures live was **not significantly different** from students who saw lectures on TV."

1968

Lange, D. L. Methods.
In E. M. Birkmaier, ed. Britannica Review of Foreign Language Education, Vol. 1, 281-310
Chicago, IL: Encyclopedia Britannica

1968

Mielke, K.
Questioning the Questions of ETV Research
Educational Broadcasting Review

1968

Thornton, J. W. and Brown, J. W.
New Media & College Teaching: Instructional Television
NEA (National Education Association): Department of Audiovisual Instruction

1968

Travers, R. M. W.
Theory of Perception and the Design of Audiovisual Materials
Paper presented at the faculty on educational media, Apr. 22
Bucknell University; Lewisburg, PA

1969

Davis, R., Johnson, C., Dietrich, J.
Students Attitudes, Motivations Shown to Influence Reception to Televised Lectures
College and University Business,
Vol. 46, No. 5, 59-63

"We started with some promising results that led us to the conclusion that face-to-face instruction is better than televised instruction. However, when we turned attention to variations in the television medium we discovered that the apparent reason for the face-to-face instructional superiority lay in the distinct inferiority of two-way television instruction. When we limited attention only to one-way television instruction it was **not demonstrably inferior** to face-to-face teaching. We found nothing in our analysis by teaching methods and subject matter taught that led us to a conclusion other than there was no measurable difference between the two media."

"To our initial surprise and later disappointment we found over and over again that there were **"no significant differences" (NSD)** between television and conventional instruction."

"...found **no significant differences** in males between the single-image and multi-image presentations at any achievement level, and the only female group to demonstrate any significant difference were the low achievers."

"There was **no difference** in achievement between groups."

1969
Dubin, R. & Hedley, R. A.
The Medium May Be Related to the Message
2, 16
University of Oregon; Eugene, OR

1969
Kittross, J. M.
The Farther Vision-Educational Television Today: Chapter 14 Meaningful Research in ETV
University of Wisconsin; Madison, WI

1969
Lombard, E. S.
Multi-channel, Multi-image Teaching of Synthesis Skills in Eleventh-Grade U. S. History
Unpublished Doctoral Dissertation
University of Southern California; Los Angeles, CA

1969
Madson, M. L.
Methods Including CCTV, of Presenting Introductory Biology: Their "Affect" on College Freshmen
University of Minnesota, Minneapolis, MN

"...provided taped lectures, tape recorders, and printed notes to 209 college students. Another 408 students attended regular lectures. Overall there was **no significant difference**."

1969

Menne, J. W., Klingenschmidt, J. E. & Nord, D. L.
The Feasibility of Using Taped Lectures to Replace Class Attendance
Paper presented at the annual meeting of American Educational Research Association Los Angeles, CA

"...in almost 90 percent of the comparisons there were **no substantial differences** in achievement or information gain [with media] over conventional instruction...Students learn about as well irrespective of the methods employed."

1969

Twyford, L. C.
Educational Communications Media
Encyclopedia of Educational Research, p. 370

"...this experiment **did not produce significant statistical evidence** or conclusive answers."

1970

Bollman, C. G.
The Effect of Large-Screen Multi-Image Display of Evaluative Meaning
Dissertation Abstracts International 31 (11-A), 5924
Doctoral Dissertation
Michigan State University; East Lansing, MI

"Experimental studies comparing radio teaching with other means or media have found radio **as effective** as the so-called 'conventional methods'. Even though radio has been criticized for being only an audio medium, studies have shown that visual elements in learning are not uniformly important."

1970

Forsythe, R.
Instructional Radio An Evaluation of Instructional Technology

"...participants may favor a a live' teacher in their classroom, although research studies point out that both the televised image and live presentation are **equally effective**."

1970

Gordon, G. N.
Classroom Television: New Frontiers in ITV
New York: Hastings House

32

"...**no significant differences** between the teaching strategies, except for reading, where the traditional group outperformed the two audio-active groups."

1970

Judd, W. A., Bunderson, C. V. & Bessent, E. W.
An Investigation of the Effects of Learner Control in Computer-Assisted Instruction Prerequisite Mathematics (MATHS)
University of Texas; Austin, TX

"...found **no significant difference** between the two groups on either discrimination or pronunciation."

1970

Sisson, C. R.
The Effect of Delayed Comparison in the Language Laboratory on Phoneme Discrimination and Pronouncement Accuracy
Language Learning 26, 69-88

"...**no significant differences** between the teaching strategies, except for reading, where the traditional group outperformed the two audio-active groups."

1970

Smith, W. F.
Language Learning Laboratory
In D. L. Lange, ed. Britannica Review of Foreign Language Education, Vol. 2, 191-237
Encyclopedia Britannica, Inc.
Chicago, IL

"The predominant finding from the hundreds of evaluation studies in instructional television is its overall **equal effectiveness** when compared to face-to-face instruction."

1971

Allen, W. H.
Instructional Media Research: Past, Present, and Future
Audio-Visual Communication Review, 19(1), 5-18

"**No significant differences** were found between groups in the amount of attitudinal change elicited as a result of the presentation, or between treatment of groups relative to the cognitive learning resulting from viewing the presentations. These analyses indicated one treatment **was not significantly more effective** (or even affective) than the other in producing increases in affective or cognitive learning."

1971

Atherton, L. L.
A Comparison of Movie and Multi-Image Presentation Techniques on Affective and Cognitive Learning
Doctoral dissertation
Dissertation Abstracts International 32(6-A), 5924
Michigan State University; East Lansing, MI

"...students can **learn about as well** from television as from classroom instruction..."

1971

Johnson, L.
Cable Television and Higher Education: Two Contrasting Experiences
ERIC

1971

Sticht, T. G.
Failure to Increase Learning Using the Time Saved by the Time Compression of Speech
Journal of Educational Psychology 62, 55-59.

"...the time saved in compression was lost in elaboration, and overall comprehension was **not improved**...hearing the same text twice at double speed resulted in **no more learning** than hearing the same text at normal speed...it appears that the instructional use of compression cannot be based on efficiency arguments."

34

"Administration decisions on the use of television seem to have assigned a positive evaluation to the same **no significant differences**, deducing that, if television can perform as well as conventional instruction, it holds great potential for solving some of the logistical and personnel problems in education."

1972

Anderson, C. M.
In Search of a Visual Rhetoric for Instructional Television
Audio-Visual Communication Review, Vol. 10, No. 1

1972

Brown, J. D.
An Evaluation of the Spitz Student Response System in Teaching a Course in Logical and Mathematical Concepts
Journal of Experimental Education
40(3), 12-20
in October 1997 Ed Journal, Vol. 11 no. 10
p. j-12

"… a study of freshmen men and women in a traditional college level math course, with half of the learners using a student response system… found **no significant differences** between the two groups."

"A pilot study compared 18 control students enrolled in a regular closed-circuit television class of General Psychology with 18 experimental students who were assigned to an independent study section of General Psychology. Students in independent study viewed the TV lectures at the tape stations at their discretion and took course examinations when they felt prepared. The results **indicated no significant difference** in course achievement or attitude between the two methods of course preparation. Interaction effects between independent study vs. closed-circuit TV and three levels of scholastic ability were also **nonsignificant**."

"...found **no significant differences** in learning... learner control **does not contribute** to improved attitudes."

"Results on the conventional exam showed that the experimental group performed **as well** as the regular students."

"Students like a 'talkback' system, but seem to **learn no more with it than without it**...No learning advantage has been demonstrated for 'professional' or 'artistic' production techniques..."

1972

Dambrot, F.
General Psychology Over Closed-Circuit Television
Audio-Visual Communication Review, Vol. 20, No. 2

1972

Hoyt, D. P. & Frye, D.
The Effectiveness of Telecommunications as an Educational Delivery System
Kansas State University; Manhattan, KS

1972

Postlethwaite, S. N., Novak, J. & Murray, H. T., Jr.
The Audio-Tutorial Approach to Learning
3d ed, Burgess
Minneapolis, MN

1972

Schramm, W.
Quality in Instructional Television: What Research Says About ITV
University Press of Hawaii

"...found **no differences** between learner-control and program-control groups in student attitude toward CBI."

1973

Beard, M. H., Lorton, P. V., Searle, B. W. & Atkinson, R. C.
Comparison of Student Performance and Attitude Under Three Lesson-Selection Strategies in Computer-Assisted Instruction
California Institute of Mathematical Studies in the Social Studies
Stanford University; Stanford, CA

"...it is clear that students who receive instruction by correspondence study achieve **at least as well** as students who study by other means including classroom instruction, programmed instruction, and television or by use of kinescopes or videotape...students in correspondence courses either **matched** or slightly exceeded the achievement of students taking the same courses via different formats. Instructional methodology seemed to make **no significant difference**."

1973

Childs, G. B.
Correspondence Study: Concepts and Comments
University of Nebraska; Lincoln, NE

"...the students **learned the same amount**, as measured by test performance, whether they were taught by the videotape-discussion method or by the lecture-discussion method..."

1974

Thorman, J. H. & Amb, T.
The Video Tape Presentation versus the "Live" Presentation: Better, Worse or the Same?
Moorhead State College, Moorhead, MN

36

"...an experimental study with 80 college students to test the effect of feedback on learning. **No difference** was found in learning and retention among four treatments...There can no longer be any real doubt that children and adults learn a great amount from instructional television...The effectiveness of television has now been demonstrated...in many parts of the world, in developing as well as industrialized countries, at every level from pre-school through adult education, and with a great variety of subject matter and methods...**No difference** was found in learning and retention..."

"Comprehensive was high no matter what delivery medium was used."

"The kind of research that characterizes most of the documents purporting to examine ITV...show **no significant difference** between courses taught over television and equivalent courses given to live matched groups."

"...sixty-seven American studies of the effectiveness of correspondence education at the college, technical, and high school level...there was **no significant difference** in learning outcomes between correspondence and conventional study."

1975

Chu, G. C. & Schramm, W.
Learning From Television: What the Research Says
ERIC ED 109 985

1976

Chaiken, S. & Egly, A.
Communication Modality as a Determinant of Message Persuasiveness and Message Comprehensibility
Journal of Personality and Social Psychology
34, 605-14

1976

Gordon, G. N. Classroom Television: New *Frontiers in ITV-Research and the Wonder Drug: NSD*
Communication Arts Books, Hastings House

1976

Macken, E.
Home-Based Education
U. S. Department of Health, Education, and Welfare; Washington, DC

"...participants may favor a "live" teacher in their classroom, although research studies point out that both the televised image and live presentation are **equally effective**."

"Studies have consistently reported **achievement on performance tests was similar** regardless of the medium used...media (face-to-face versus television) were not significant factors on achievement..."

"The import of this rather impressive evidence is that distant teaching, well-conceived, well-supported with the proper media, really works. It works in developing countries or in highly industrialized ones, and at many different levels of education. Where data are available, they appear to show that students in these media-extended programs learn **at least as well as** students in the same curriculum in traditional classrooms."

"There is no statistical basis to conclude that TV itself affects learning situations or grades **positively or negatively**..."

"There were **no differences** between immediate and delayed feedback."

1977

Crow, M. L.
Teaching on Television
Faculty Development Resource Center
University of Texas; Austin, TX

1977

Saloman, G. & Clark, R. E.
Reexamining the Methodology of Research on Media & Technology in Education
Review of Educational Research

1977

Schramm, W.
Big Media Little Media
Sage Publications; Beverly Hills, CA

1977

Wood, D. M. and Wylie, D. G.
Educational Telecommunications
Belmont, CA, Wadsworth

1978

Char, R. O.
The Effect of Delay of Informative Feedback on the Retention of Verbal Information and Higher-order Learning, for College Students
Doctoral Dissertation Abstracts International 40, 748A
Florida State University; Tallahassee, FL

"...remote mediated learning combined with appropriate contact with live instructors and peers, can be at **least as effective** and significantly less costly per unit than traditional lecture modes."

"...found **no differences** between learner-control and program-control groups in student attitudes towards CBI."

"He compared achievement levels of learners taking a child development course over cable television split into two groups. One group has the ability to communicate with the instructor by using the telephone to call the instructor while the other groups had the same telephone calling capability but also had the ability to respond to questions posed by the instructor using a data response terminal... **no significant differences** in learners achievement were found."

"...**no significant differences** between information retention of jurors when television was used to present testimony \instead of direct live observation."

"... there is either **no significant difference** in achievement in comparative studies or, when there is a difference, students in televised courses generally have higher achievement rates than on-campus students in similar courses."

1978

Kelly, J. T. & Anadam, K
Nationwide Prime-Time Television in Higher Education
International Journal of Instructional Media

1978

Lahey, G. F.
Learner Control of Computer-Assisted Instruction: A Comparison to Guided Instruction
Paper presented at the annual meeting of the Association for the Development of Computer-Based Instructional Systems
Dallas, TX

1978

Lucas, W. A.
Spartanburg, S. C.: Testing the Effectiveness of Video, Voice, and Data Feedback...
Journal of Communication, 23, 168-179
October, 1997, Ed Journal, Vol. 11 No. 10, p. j-12

1978

Miller, G. R. & Fontes, N. E.
Video Technology and the Legal Powers
Sage Publications, Beverly Hills, CA

1978

Purdy, L.
Telecourse Students: How well do they learn?
Paper presented at the Annual Convention of American Association of Community and Junior Colleges
ERIC NO. ED 154851; Atlanta, GA

"In four cases the visual component of television was not being used and did not appear to be needed. If the television receiver were replaced by radio it appears **unlikely** that the measured **learning outcomes would be appreciably effected**."

"...overall difference in achievement had no practical significance because **no significant difference** in achievement was found in thirty-two studies."

"In terms of academic achievement there were **no significant differences** between the groups."

"… there was **no significant difference in** achievement between [sic] the three groups."

"The results of several decades of research...can be summed up as **no significant difference**."

1978

Tiffon, J. W.
Problems in Instructional Television in Latin America
Revista de Tendogia Educativa 4(2), 163-234

1979

Orlansky, S. and String, J.
Cost-Effectiveness of Computer-Based Education in Military Training
IDA paper, Science, and Technical Division
Institute for Defense Analysis
Arlington, VA

1979

Sakamoto, T.
Utilization of Educational Technology in Higher Education of Japan
The Pursuit of Excellence in Higher Education
Keinyong University, Korea

1980

Hult, R. E.
The Effectiveness of University Television Instruction and Factors Influencing Student Attitudes
College Student Journal, 14(1), 5-7
October 1997 Ed Journal, Vol. 11 No. 10, p. j-5

1980

Wilkenson, G. L.
Media in Instruction: 60 Years of Research
AECT & NAVA

"...students learned slightly more from visual-based instruction than from traditional teaching, but there was typically **no difference** between the two groups in regard to course completion, student attitudes, or the correlation between attitudes and achievement."

"...conducted a series of televised lectures on identical subject matter in a similar situation...(1) with the professor's face on one TV monitor and two types of instructional material on the other two...(2) with any two TV images frozen...and any single moving image...(3) with no professor's face but two types of instructional material on two TV monitors...There were **no significant differences** in academic achievement among the three groups."

"...students learned **at least as well** as resident students..."

"Telidon instruction was **as effective** the traditional correspondence and conventional in-school instruction."

"In general, comparisons of learning from audio and print have shown **no difference...no differences** for children...**no advantage** with children for print plus audio over either print or audio alone."

1981

Cohen, P., Ebeling, B. & Kulik, J.
A Meta-Analysis of Outcome Studies of Visual-based Instruction
Educational Communications and Technology Journal

1981

Sakamoto, T.
Innovations in Higher Education
Research Institute for Higher Education
Hiroshima University; Hiroshima, Japan

1982

Christopher, G. R.
The Air Force Institute of Technology - the Air Force Reaches Out Through Media: An Update
University of Wisconsin; Madison, WI

1982

Montgomerie, T. C.
Telidon Distance Education Field Trial
Telidon Project Evaluation
Department of Education, Planning and Research Branch, November, 207 _____
Alberta, Canada

1982

Nugent, G. C.
Pictures, Audio, and Print: Symbolic Representation and Effect on Learning
Educational Communication and Technology Journal 30, 163-74

"...overall [24 years], there was **no statistically significant difference** in the academic performance of the two groups..."

"...there are no learning benefits to be gained from employing any specific medium to deliver instruction...The best current evidence is that media are mere vehicles that deliver instruction but **do not influence** student achievements any more than the truck that delivers our groceries causes changes in our nutrition."

"...audioconferencing with an existing nursing school...and videotapes of...classes were combined...there were **also no significant differences** in course grades or scores on national nursing tests..."

"...academic achievement and student satisfaction in teleconferencing classes **is equal** to that of students in resident classes."

"In each instance **no difference** was found in the amount of learning that occurred between telecourse students and on-campus students."

1983

Allen, M. L.
Paper Presented to ASEE at the Arizona State Interactive Video Experience
Arizona State University; Tempe, AZ

1983

Clark, R. E.
Reconsidering Research on Learning from Media
Review of Educational Research 53 (4), 445-59

1983

Holdampf, B. A.
Innovative Associate Degree Nursing Program-Remote Area
Department of Occupational Education and Technology
Texas Education Agency

1983

Kruh, J.
Student Evaluation of Instructional Teleconferencing
Parker & C. Olgren, eds. Teleconferencing and Electronic Communications, Vol. 2
University of Wisconsin-Extension
Center for Interactive Programs
Madison, WI

1983

Smith, J.
Evaluation of the Telecourse Program at Saddleback College: Student Retention and Academic Achievement
Nova University, Fort Lauderdale, FL

"Results indicated that **neither** timing of feedback nor type of feedback **made any significant difference** between groups."

1983

Wager, S. U.
The Effect of Immediacy and Type of Informative Feedback on Retention in a Computer-Assisted Task
(Doctoral Dissertation, Florida State University)
Dissertation Abstracts International 44, 2100A

"...found **no significant difference** (NSD) in learning."

1984

Chute, A. G., Bruning, K. K., & Hulick, M. K.
The AT&T Communications National Teletraining Network: Applications, Benefits and Costs
Cincinnati, OH: AT&T Communications Sales and Marketing Education

"...achievement scores were **at least as high** on materials presented over two-way television as they were on materials presented with the professor present \in the classroom."

1984

Denton, J. J., et al.
An Examination of Instructional Strategies Used with Two-Way Television
Texas A&M University; College Station, TX

"...studies indicate **little or no difference** in learner outcomes when various media are compared."

1984

Herschback, D.
Addressing Vocational Training and Retraining Through Educational Technology: Policy Alternatives, (No. 276)
Columbus, Ohio

"Nurses had **comparable achievement** regardless of the medium."

1984

Kuramoto, A.
Teleconferencing for Nurses: Evaluating Its Effectiveness
Teleconferencing and Electronic Communications III
University of Wisconsin; Madison, WI

"...student achievement was **comparable** to achievement resulting from resident instruction."

1984

Partin, G. & Atkins, E.
Teaching via the Electronic Blackboard
Teleconferencing and Electronic Communications IV, 68-73

"...telecourses are **at least as good** as traditional on-campus lecture format courses."

1984

Smith, J.
An Evaluation of Telecourse Achievement at Saddleback College
Technological Horizons in Education, 11(1), 94-96

"...1: there is no evidence to support the idea that face-to-face instruction is the optimum delivery method, 2: Instruction by teleconferencing can facilitate learning **as well as** or better than can classroom instruction, and 3: the absence of face-to-face contact is **not detrimental** to the learning process."

1984

Weingand, D. E.
Telecommunications and the Traditional Classroom: A Study of the Delivery of Education
University of Wisconsin; Madison, WI

"Media are primarily for the delivery and storage of information. Media do not directly determine the type or amount of learning. It is **the messages themselves**, which are carried by media, that are critical factors for producing achievement or changing attitudes."

1984

Winn, W.
Why Media?
Instructional Innovator

"...performance **does not significantly differ** between telecourse and classroom students taking equivalent courses."

1984

Zigerell, J.
Distance Education: An Information Age Approach to Adult Education
ERIC Clearinghouse on Adult, Career, and Vocational Education
Columbus, Ohio

"Learning under the two lectures modes was **statistically equivalent** and class attendance was unaffected by the mode of instruction."

1985

Ellis, L. & Mathis, D.
College Students Learning from Televised versus Conventional Classroom Lectures: A Controlled Experiment

"...while the interactive technology, as noted earlier, offers interesting potential, interactive video **differs little** from the allied technology from either learning or cognitive perspectives."

1985

Hannafin, M. J.
Empirical Issues in the Study of Computer-Assisted Interactive Video
ECTJ 33(4), 235-47

"...**no significant difference** in student satisfaction between a telephone-based course and a face-to-face course."

1985

Kirkhorn, J.
A Teletraining Study: Student Learning Preferences
University of Wisconsin; Madison, WI

"There were **no significant differences** between feedback levels, suggesting that more-complex feedback **did not prove more effective** in either task. An additional finding was that there were **no differences** between feedback that was given immediately or feedback that was delayed."

1985

Lee, O. M.
The Effect of Type of Feedback on Rule Learning in Computer-based Instruction
Doctoral Dissertation
Florida State University; Tallahassee, FL
Dissertation Abstracts International 46, 955A

"In some instances students recorded gains larger than the on-campus students; However, in general the results indicated **no significant differences**."

1985

Michael, W. B. & Knapp-Lee, L.
Evaluating Learning in Telecourses
Coastline Community College;
Fountain Valley, CA

"Teachers and administrators in Iowa's two-way interactive television (TWIT) project found **no significant differences** between TWIT classes and other sections of the same class taught face-to-face by the same teacher."

1985

Nelson, R. N.
Two-Way Microwave Transmission Consolidates Improves Education
NASSP Bulletin

"...found **no differences** between low- and high-reading ability groups in any type of options selected."

1985

Reinking, D. & Schreiner, R.
The Effects of Computer-Mediated Text on Measures of Reading Comprehension and Reading Behavior
Reading Research Quarterly 22(5), 536-52

"...performance level *equaled* that experienced in other on-campus courses. This finding held true for students in both two-year and four-year institutions."

1985

Research Communications, Ltd.
Research on Student Uses of the Annenberg/ CPB Telecourses for the Fall of 1984

"...students in remote interactive television classes *achieved as well* on post-tests as did students in traditional classrooms."

1985

Robinson, R.
An Investigation of Technical Innovation: Interactive T.V.
AECT

"Students in interactive-television classes *achieved as well* on the post-test as did students in 'live' classrooms."

1985

Robinson, R. S., Collins, K. M. & West, P. C.
Share Advanced [Secondary] Courses With Other Schools via Interactive Cable Television
Northern Illinois University

"...students can learn just **as well,** if not better from television...There is a good deal of research which suggests that content may be learned just **as well** through television as through print."

1986

Bates, A. W.
Learning From Television
Open Learning for Adults
Longmans

"...students **learn as well** in distance education programs as they do in regular programs..."

1986

Bates, A. W. & Couell, R. N.
Distance Education: An Overview
Northwest Regional Educational Laboratory

"Television instruction is **neither superior nor inferior** to traditional classroom presentation. The question is not which medium works best, but what is effective instruction?"

1986

Bergin, V.
Letter to Nil Whittingham, June 5
(unpublished)

"The study concluded that while tele-course students might not have liked some aspects of the telecourse as well as the more traditional delivery modes, they **performed as well** as day and evening students on traditional tests."

"...research conducted by Sales and Marketing Education Division has shown teletraining was **as effective** and in some cases more effective than face-to-face instruction. In general, there were **no significant differences** between the amount of information students learned in classes that were teletrained and the amount they learned in face-to-face instruction."

"Were the "live" and "TV" groups different in course performance or attitudes? The data...indicate that they were not; statistical tests (t-tests, Chi-square) applied to all...items showed **no significant differences** (at the p is less than or equal to .05 level) between the responses in 'live' sections and 'TV' sections...When we conduct telephone surveys in several courses and statistical tests on the data **no significant difference** between 'TV' and 'live' groups, we conclude that students can learn as well as they learn with professors present."

1986

Carvalho, G. F., Graham, G. H. & Gray, M. A.
An Evaluation of Telecourse Delivery of a Basic Management Class: A Comparison of Performance and Attitudes with Day and Evening Sections
Wichita State University; Wichita, KS
and Beech Aircraft Corporation

1986

Chute, A. G., Hulick, M., Messmer, C., Hancock, P.
Teletraining in the Corporate Environment Teleconferencing and Electronic Communications
University of Wisconsin; Madison, WI

1986

Creswell, K. W.
Does Instructional TV Make the Grade?
Journal of Educational Television,
Vol. 12, No. 1

"...there is **no distinct advantage** to one medium over another."

1986

Hoko, A.
What Is the Scientific Value of Comparing Automated and Human Instruction?
Educational Technology 26(2), 18

"...students taught under TJaLP can learn as well as those taught in the regular classroom...**no statistical significance** emerged between the two groups..."

1986

Kataoka, H. C.
Televised Japanese Language Program: The First Year
Foreign Language Annuals, Vol. 19, No. 6

(48) "...faculty reported that telecourse students performed better than or **as well** as non-telecourse students..."

1986

LaRose, R.
Adoption of Telecourses: The Adoption and Utilization of Annenberg/CPB Project Telecourses
The ELRA Group, Incorporated

"...there were **no substantive differences** in achievement or cost effectiveness among the various media."

1986

McClelland, J. Saeed, F.
Adult Education and Vocational Education: Implications for Research on Distance Delivery
Minnesota Research and Development Center, University of Minnesota; Minneapolis, MN
(ERIC Document No. ED276852)

"...student achievement **has been consistent** with that experienced in traditional classes."

1986

Pease, P.
The Evaluation of the TI-IN Network's Satellite-Based Education Network: A Preliminary Report TI-IN Network, 3 June

"There are **no significant differences** in graduate performance between traditional and video-based degree students..."

1986

Stone, H. R.
Non-Tutored Video Instruction in Graduate Engineering Education
University of Massachusetts; Amherst, MA

"...there were **no significant differences** between groups."

1986

Sutliff, R.
Effect of Adjunct Postquestions on Achievement
Journal of Industrial Teacher Education
23(3), 45-54

"...for the spring semester, **no significant differences** in learning are found between the groups..."

1987

Grimes, P. W., Niss, J. & Nielsen, J.
An Evaluation of Learning & Attitudinal Changes of Students in Economics USA
The Annenberg/CPB Project

"...**no statistically significant differences**...TJaLP students can learn Japanese as well as students in regular classes...performance is not lower."

1987

Kataoka, H. C.
Long-Distance Language Learning: The Second Year of Televised Japanese
North Carolina State University; Raleigh, NC

"...in a wide range of elective programming provided from 1983 to 1986, **no statistically significant differences** in achievement were found between students taking courses traditionally or by..."

1987

Kitchen, W.
Education & Telecommunications: Partners in-Progress
Testimony before the U. S. Senate Committee on Labor & Human Services

"...the pattern of scores across seven courses justifies the conclusion that receiving (distant) students do at **least as well** and perhaps better than their sending-site counterparts and nonteleteaching control students."

1987

Murray, J. & Heil, M.
Project Evaluation: 1986-87 Pennsylvania Teleteaching Project
Mansfield University of Pennsylvania; Mansfield, PA

"Evaluations to date of the effectiveness of this kind of distance learning show **no significant differences** when compared with traditional in-class instruction."

1987

Timpson, W. & Jones, C.
Distance Learning via Technology
The Gifted Child Today, 12, 10-11

"All of the research published since 1920 has indicated that correspondence students perform just **as well** as, and in most cases better than, their classroom counterparts."

1987

Valore, L. & Diehl, G.
The Effectiveness and Acceptance of Home Study
National Home Study Council
Washington DC

1987

Whittington, N.
Is Instructional Television Educationally Effective? A Research Review
The American Journal of Distance Education, 1, 47-57

"...a three-year study...which compared the performance of full-time Stanford students and students obtaining instruction via the live, interactive ITFS system...16,652 students taking traditional, on-campus instruction scored a mean GPA of 3.40, while 1,771 students taking live, interactive video instruction has a mean GPA of 3.39. In addition...Stanford is using tutored video instruction...Research indicates that this method...also promoted **equivalent student achievement**..."

"...television-delivered instruction is equivalent to traditional, classroom-based instruction in its learning effectiveness... outcomes of the television courses are **roughly equivalent** to the outcomes of the comparable traditional courses...telecourse students performed better than or as well as non-telecourse students...a third of the faculty studied reported that Annenberg/CPB courses retained more students than traditionally taught courses. Another third said that retention was equal to traditionally taught courses."

1988

Annenberg/CPB Project
Teaching Telecourses: Opportunities and Options: How Do Telecourses Compare to Other Types of Courses?
PBS Adult Learning Service

50

"...video can be **just as effective** or more effective than other forms of instruction."

1988

Atherton, J. & Buriak, P.
Video Simulation as a Computer Applications Instructional Technique for Professionals and Students
Journal of Vocational Education Research
Vol. 13, No. 3, 59-71

"Students appeared to learn from the teletraining mode **as well as**, if not better than, they did from the face-to-face mode."

1988

Chute, A. G., Balthazar, L. B. & Posten, C. O.
Learning from Tele-training
The American Journal of Distance Education,
Vol. 2, No. 3

"**No significant difference** rates resulted for any feedback group...Type of feedback made no difference in the number of errors during instruction."

1988

Dempsey, J. V.
The Effects of Four Methods of Immediate Feedback on Retention, Discrimination Error, and Feedback Study Time in Computer-Based Instruction
Doctoral Dissertation, Dissertation Abstracts International 49, 1434A
Florida State University; Tallahassee, FL

"...the combined data show that the ITV method was **at least as good** as live instruction."

1988

Gibbons, J. F.
Tutored Videotape Instruction: An Approach to Educational Productivity
Stanford University; Stanford, CA

"...**neither** distant learner group **experienced a significant change** in their attitudes towards economics. **No significant difference** is found between the off-campus and long-distance groups...**no significant differences** were uncovered between either of the distance learner groups exposed to "Economics USA" and the control group."

1988

Grimes, P. W., Neilsen, J. E. & Niss, J. F.
The Performance of Nonresident Students in the "Economics USA" Telecourse
The American Journal of Distance Education,
Vol. 2, No. 2, 36-41

"...found **no differences** between learner-control and program-control groups in student attitude toward CBI."

"...**no significant differences** between on-campus and off-campus degree students regarding performance."

"**No significant data** was found to indicate that school-wide student test scores have been affected by the kind of intensity of CAI that occurs in most elementary school settings."

"...there was **no statistically significant difference** between the mean score achieved by students who received instruction from the Instructional Media Utilization Package and...by students who received only classroom instruction..."

"The research base, though scant at present, suggests the students who study via telecommunicated distance education approaches **perform as well** as their counterparts in traditional classroom settings..."

1988

Kinzie, M. B., Sullivan, H. J. & Berdel, R. L.
Learner Control and Achievement in Science Computer-Assisted Instruction
Journal of Educational Psychology 83(3), 140-46

1988

Stone, H. R.
Variations in Characteristics & Performance Between On-Campus & Video-based Off-Campus Engineering Graduate Students
University of Massachusetts; Amherst, MA

1988

Tso, A.
Computer-Based Instruction Delivery Systems Educational Resources and Techniques
Texas Association for Educational Technology Journal

1988

Woodward, D. B.
Teaching Instructional Media Utilization: Video Tape Package vs. Classroom Instruction
Illinois State University; Normal, IL

1989

Barker, B. O., Frisbie, G. and Patrick, K. R.
Broadening the Definition of Distance Education in Light of the New Telecommunications Technologies
The American Journal of Distance Education, Vol. 3, No. 1, 20-27

"Most students (53.8 percent) felt that televised instruction via satellite maintained their interest **as well as** did regular classroom instruction."

1989

Barker, B. O. & Platten, M. R.
Student Perceptions on the Effectiveness of College Credit Courses Taught via Satellite
Readings in Distance Learning and Instruction No. 2, 104-110
Pennsylvania State University; University Park, PA

1989

Beare, P. L.
The Comparative Effectiveness of Videotape, Audiotape, & Telelectures in Delivering Continuing Teacher Education
The American Journal of Distance Education, 3(2), 57-66

"...individual instructional formats **had little effect** on student achievement or course evaluation...the lack of individual opportunity to interact on a daily basis with the instructor did not reduce student learning...**no differences** on student achievement or course evaluations."

"Students appeared to learn from the teletraining mode **as well**, if not better, than they did from the face-to-face mode."

1989

Chute, A. G., Balthazar, & Poston, C. O.
Learning from Teletraining
Readings in Distance Learning and Instruction No. 2, 87-96
Pennsylvania State University; University Park, PA

"...listed a half-dozen studies from [the 1930s and 1940s] which demonstrated **no difference** in student performance between those who listened to radio lectures and those who attended live classes."

1989

Gibbons, M.
The Effectiveness of Technology Applied to Instruction: A Summary of the Research Literature
San Diego State University; San Diego, CA

"...**no significant differences** were uncovered between either of the distant learner groups exposed to "Economics USA" and the control group."

1989

Grimes, P. W., Nielsen, J. E. and Niss, J. F.
The Performance of Nonresident Students in the "Economics USA" Telecourse
Readings in Distance Learning
Pennsylvania State University; University Park, PA

"...**no reliable differences** between task conditions for the three groups...there were **no significant differences** in task performance between groups."

1989

Hammond, N. & Allison, L.
The Travel Metaphor as Design Principle and Training Aid for Navigating Around Complex Systems
Diaper & R. Winder, eds. People and Computers III, Cambridge, England
Cambridge University Press

"**No significant differences** were observed in terms of performance on the incidental learning questions."

1989

Jones, T.
Incidental Learning During Information Retrieval: A Hypertext Experiment
Maurer, ed. Computer-Assisted Learning, 235-51
Springer; Berlin, Germany

"...**no differences** on achievement-per-time-spent between self-paced and lesson-paced interactive video formats."

1989

Lopez, C. L. & Harper, M.
The Relationship Between Learner Control of CAI and Locus of Control Among Hispanic Students
Educational Technology Research and Development 37(4), 19-28

"Studies completed during the past three decades indicate **performances** by students on achievement-type tests are similar regardless of instruction proximity...comparable performance can be expected from students."

1989

Ritchie, H. & Newby, J.
Classroom Lecture/Discussion vs. Live Televised Instruction: A Comparison of Effects on Student Performance, Attitudes, & Interaction
American Journal of Distance Education

"The students who saw the lessons on tape felt they did not learn the material as well as they would have in a traditional classroom setting. However, their test scores were **not significantly different** from those of the traditionally-taught group."

1989

Russell, T. L.
A Study of Foreign Language Instruction via TOTE
Research in Distance Education, Vol. 1, No. 2, 2-4

"...the grade performance of the on-campus student is **statistically indistinguishable** from that of the off-campus TV student."

"...**no significant differences** in the achievement or attitudes of students receiving live classroom instruction and those receiving some type of tele-vised instruction. Overall, **no significant differences** were found in the achievement levels...**no significant differences** in end of course grades between ITV and non-ITV classes...no significant differences in grades between the origination site and remote sites...students **do equally well** in courses taught over the ITV system as they do in a traditional classroom setting. Students learned course content generally well... Students receiving their course instruction by means of interactive television learned as well as students in a traditional classroom."

"...an examination of the students' grades indicates **no apparent advantage** at all..."

"Evaluations to date of the effective-ness of this kind of distance learning show **no significant differences** when compared with traditional in-class instruction."

1989

Seigel, A. E. & Davis, C.
Delivering Undergraduate Engineering Courses on Television: How Do Grades Compare?
University of Maryland; College Park, MD

1989

Silvernail, D. L. & Johnson, J. L.
Evaluative Research Studies of the University of Southern Maine Instructional Television System
University of Maine; Orono, ME

1989

Timmons, K.
Educational Effectiveness of Various Adjuncts to Printed Study Material in Distance Education
Research in Distance Education, Vol. 1, No. 3, 12-13

1989

Timpson, W. & Jones, C.
Distance Learning via Technology
The Gifted Child Today, 12, 10-11

"...students taking courses via television achieve, in most cases, **as well** as students taking courses via traditional methods...Television is a technological device for transmitting communication and has no intrinsic effect, for good or ill, on student achievement. Effective instructional design and techniques are the crucial elements in student achievement whether instruction is delivered by television or by traditional means."

"...although it was predicted that learners would perceive that they invested more mental effort in processing the IV lesson than in processing the ITV lessons and TV lesson, and that learners would perceive that they invested more mental effort in processing an ITV lesson than in processing a TV lesson, there was **no significant difference** between the three groups."

"...**no differences** on achievement-per-time-spent between self-paced and lesson-paced interactive video formats."

"... **no differences** in learner achievement bet\ween groups..."

1989

Whittington, N.
Is Instructional Television Educationally Effective? A Research Review
Readings in Principles of Distance Education
Pennsylvania State University; University Park, PA

1990

Cennamo, K. S. Squenye, Smith, P. L.
Can Interactive Video Overcome the "Couch Potato" Syndrome?
AECT National Conversion Research and Theory Proceedings

1990

Dalton, D. W.
The Effects of Cooperative Learning Strategies on Achievement and Attitudes During Interactive Video
Journal of Computer-Based Instruction 17(1), 8-16

1990

Garvin-Kester, B.J.
The Effect of a Student Response Systems Questions on Learner Attention and Performance in a Distance Learning Environment
Doctoral Dissertation
Northern Illinois University; De Kalb, IL
D.A.I. 52/02-A, 392

"The evaluation found that...there were **no differences** between resident and ACC students on objective performance measures."

"...research continues to indicate there is **no significant difference** in what students learn whether they are in large or small classes, participating in telephone or video conferences, or studying alone in an independent study course."

"The students at the remote sites received grades an average of .01 lower on a 4.0 scale than students at the origination sites. This was not a **significant difference**."

"...good teaching by teleconferencing and other distance education techniques has results **no better or worse** than good teaching by any other method, including good face-to-face instruction."

"There was **no significant difference** in students' mean performance scores...there were **no significant differences** between groups on their evaluation of instructor..."

1990

Hahn, H.
Distributed Training for the Reserve Component: Remote Delivery Using Asynchronous Computer Conferencing Report
No. 2Q263743A794
Boise ID: Army Research Institute

1990

Huffington, D. D., Young, R. C.
Integrating Video Technology into Independent Study: The Missouri Experience
The American Journal of Distance Education, Vol. 4, No. 2

1990

Kabat, E. J., Friedel, J. N.
The Eastern Iowa Community College Districts Televised Interactive Education Evaluation Report
Eastern Iowa Community College, Clinton, IA

1990

Moore, M. G., Thompson, M. M.
The Effects of Distance Learning: A Summary of Literature
American Center for the Study of Distance Education

1990

Pirrong, G. D., Lathen, W. C.
The Use of Interactive Television in Business Education
Educational Technology
May, 49-54

chronological listing of entries

"There were very small, **nonsignificant differences** in course outcomes between the two groups, and there were no differences between the two groups in the number of course failures."

"Student performance on examinations was **comparable** in originating and remote classrooms, and student attitudes were **similar** at both sites."

"Color seems not to increase learning...Students like a talk-back system but seem to **learn no more** with it than without it...**No learning advantage** has been demonstrated for "professional" or "artistic" production techniques...Eye contact seems not to contribute to learning...adding humor adds not to learning effect."

"...students **do not suffer** from the inability to talk back to faculty in real time...distance students perform better where they control not only where but when learning occurs."

"...the technology chosen **may not affect** the eventual achievement outcome, but it greatly affects the efficiency with which instruction can be delivered."

1990

Rupinski, T., Stoloff, P.
An Evaluation of Navy Video Teletraining (VTT), CRM 90-36
Center for Naval Analyses
Alexandria, VA

1990

Simpson, H., Pugh, H., Parchman, S.
A Two-Point Video-Teletraining System: Design, Development, and Evaluation
Navy Personnel R&D Center
Technical Report-90-5

1990

Stone, H. R.
Candid Classroom ITV: An Evaluation of its Effectiveness
University of Delaware; Newark, DE

1990

Stone, H. R.
Does Interactivity Matter in Video-Based Off-Campus Graduate Engineering Education?
University of Delaware; Newark, DE

1990

Winn, B.
Media and Instructional Methods
D. R. Garrison & D. Shale, eds
Education at a Distance: From Issues to Practice, 53-66
Krieger; Malabar, Florida

"...**no significant differences** between the treatment groups examined in the study. Further, at the end of the course, there were **no significant differences** among the groups in attitude toward the subject matter."

"... **no significant differences** in academic performance and only a few differences in learner attitudes."

"Historically, the introduction of each new medium of instruction is accompanied by research designed to determine if it is as effective as traditional instruction...Each new wave of comparison studies brings similar results - **no significant difference**..."

"One of the first issues to be investigated was whether students were getting the same education in the technologically delivered classes as in the traditional classroom...there are **no significant differences** in academic performance for students in the two settings."

"**No significant differences** (p.01) were found between the students in origination sites and those in receive sites."

1991

Cheng, H. C., Lehman, J. and Armstrong, P.
Comparison of Performance and Attitude in Traditional and Computer Conferencing Classes
The American Journal of Distance Education
5(3), 51-64

1991

Chung, J.
Televised Teaching Effectiveness: Two Case Studies
Educational Technology, 31, 41-47
October 1997 Ed Journal, Vol.11 No.10, j4-9

1991

Dillon, C. L. & Harwell, D.
Telecommunications in Oklahoma: A Summary of Research
The University of Oklahoma; Norman, OK

1991

Gehlauf, D. N., Shatz, M. A. & Frye, T. W.
Faculty Perceptions of Interactive Instructional Strategies: Implications for Training
The American Journal of Distance Education,
Vol. 5, No. 3

1991

Johnson, J. L.
Evaluation Report of the Community College of Maine Interactive Television System
University of Southern Maine; Portland, ME

"The conclusions reached by these studies agreed that, at worst, there were **no significant differences** in learning achievement between televisual and traditional classroom instruction."

1991

Johnstone, S. M.
Research on Telecommunicated Learning: Past, Present, and Future
The Annuals of the American Academy of Political and Social Science, 514, 49-57
Ed Journal, October, 1991, Vol. 11 No. 10, p.j-4

"...there were **no significant differences** in achievement between students using only videodisc and students using videotape-based units."

1991

McNeill, B. J., Nelson, K. R.
Meta-analysis of Interactive Video Instruction: A Ten-Year Review of Achievement Effects
Journal of Computer-Based Instruction, Vol. 18, No. 1, 1-6

60

"Test scores, completion rates, student perceptions, and costs were compared to resident training, and results of instruction by CMC were found to be **no different** from that of resident instruction."

1991

Phelps, R. H., Wells, R. A., Ashworth, R. L., Jr., Hahn, H. A.
Effectiveness and Costs of Distance Education Using Computer-Mediated Communication
American Journal of Distance Education, 5(3), 7-19

"...found **no differences** between learner-control and program-control groups in student attitude toward CBI."

1991

Pridemore, D. R. & Klein, J. D.
Control of Feedback in Computer-Assisted Instruction
Educational Technology Research and Development 39(4), 27-32

"...student achievement was higher and **comparable** to live instruction with fully-interactive VTT... Student achievement was **not higher** in the two-way video class when compared to the one-way video class..."

1991

Simpson, H., Pugh, H. & Parchman, S.
Empirical Comparison of Alternative Video Training Technologies
Technical Report-92-3
Navy Personnel R&D Center
San Diego, California

"...**no difference** in knowledge gained when compared to other methods of instruction."

Thomas, R. & Hooper, E.
Simulations: An Opportunity We Are Missing
Journal of Research on Computing in
Education
Vol. 13, No. 4, 497-513

1991

"...compared the effectiveness of a hypertext document containing material on introductory statistics and hypothesis testing...there were **no significant differences** in the objective performances of the groups."

van den Berg, S. & Watt, J. H.
Effects of Educational Setting on Student
Responses to Structured Hypertext
Journal of Computer-Based Instruction 18(4),
118-24

⊢⊢⊢⊢⊢ 61 ⊣

1992

"...found **no differences** between learner-control and program-control groups in student attitude toward CBI."

Armone, M. P. & Grabowski, B. L.Effects on
Childrens' Achievement and Curiosity of
Variations in Learner Control Over an
Interactive Video Lesson
Educational Technology Research and
Development 40(1), 15-27

1992

"...**no significant differences** between the audio and the traditional [face-to-face] group in either restricted or expanded thinking questions...no significant differences between the audio and the audio video group, or between the audio and the traditional group."

Bauer, J. W., Rezabek, L. L.
The Effects of Two-Way Visual Contact on
Student Verbal Interactions During
Teleconferenced Instruction
AECT National Convention Research & Theory
Proceedings

1992

"... **no differences** in perception of course content or instructional delivery methods based on the site of the learners... **no differences** in learner outcomes, while the grade distribution was reported as typical for a graduate engineering class."

Britton, O. L.
Interactive Distance Education in Higher
Education and the Impact of Delivery Styles
on Student Perceptions
Doctoral Dissertation
Wayne State University; Detroit, MI
D.A.I. 53/ 12-A, 4223

"**Few found significant differences** in learning benefit..."

1992

Dillon, C. L., Walsh, S.
The Comparative Learning Benefit of One-way and Two-way Videoconferencing for Distance Education Applications
The University of Oklahoma; Norman, OK

"There were **no significant differences** in reading achievement between the two groups."

1992

Figueroa, M. L.
Understanding Students Approaches to Learning in University Traditional and Distance Education Courses
Journal of Distance Education, 7(3), 15-28

"… there were **no significant differences in** learning between the two groups at any level or instructional strategy."

1992

Haynes, J. M., Dillon, C.
Distance Education: Learning Outcomes, Interaction, and Attitudes
Journal of Education for Library and Information Science, 33 (1), 35-45

"When these elaborations were embedded in the CAI training...there were **no differences** between the learner-generated or experimenter-provided elaborations."

1992

Johnsey, A., Morrison, G. R., Ross, S. M.
Using Elaboration Strategies Training in Computer-Based Instruction to Promote Generative Learning
Contemporary Educational Psychology 17, 125-35

"...distance education **is effective** when effectiveness is measured by achievement, by attitudes, and by cost effectiveness... Student achievement in interactive distance education classes has been **as good** as or better than that of students learning from traditional teaching methods."

1992

Jones, J. I., Simonson, M., Kemis, M., Sorensen, C.
Distance Education: A Cost Analysis
Iowa State University of Science and Technology; Ames, IA

1992

"… there was **no difference** in learning outcome between the origination site and the remote with two-way video and two-way audio."

Nixon, D. E.
Simulteaching Access to Learning by Means of Interactive Television
Community/Junior College Quarterly,
16, 167-175

1992

"Most studies comparing traditional classroom instruction with ITV have shown **no significant differences** in student achievement…instructional television appears to produce comparable academic achievement to traditional classroom instruction."

Olcott, D.
Instructional Television: A Review of Selected Evaluation Research
Oregon State University; Corvallis, OR

1992

"No matter how it is produced, how it is delivered, whether or not it is interactive, low-tech or high-tech, students **learn equally well** with each technology and learn **as well as** their on-campus, face-to-face counterparts…"

Russell, T. L.
Television's Indelible Impact on Distance Education: What We Should Have Learned from Comparative Research
Research in Distance Education, October, Vol. 4, No. 4, 2-4

1992

"…found **no differences** between learner-control and program-control groups in student attitude toward CBI."

Shyu, H.-Y. & Brown, S. W
Learner Control Versus Program Control in Interactive Videodisc Instruction: What Are the Effects in Procedural Learning?
International Journal of Instructional Media
19(2), 85-96

"...observations indicated that the learning processes occurring in the off-line laboratories were **very similar** to those in traditional resident laboratories."

1992

Simpson, H., Pugh, H., Parchman, S.
Use of Video-Teletraining to Deliver Hands-on Training: Concept Test and Evaluation, TN-92-14
Navy Personnel R&D Center; San Diego, CA

"Many media practitioners who had a professional interest in demonstrating the superiority of mediated instruction were stunned to read that research indicated that instructional media were **not inherently 'better'**...The literature clearly demonstrates that for every study that shows the new medium is better, another study shows the opposite."

1992

Thompson, A. D., Simonson, M. R., Hargrave, C. P.
Educational Technology: A Review of the Research Associate for Educational Communications and Technology

"Statistical analysis of the data showed that there was **no difference** in performance of the two skills between those who received in-class instruction and those who received instruction through video conferencing."

1992

Williams, A. T.
The Efficacy of Premium Broadband Video Conferencing in Teaching Cardiac Arrest Skills: A Comparative Study, Dissertation
Columbia Pacific University, Canaca

"**No significant differences** in retention rates resulted for any feedback group...Type of feedback made **no difference** in the number of errors during instruction."

1993

Dempsey, J. V., Driscoll, M. P., Litchfield, B. C.
Feedback, Retention, Discrimination Error, and Feedback Study Time
Journal of Research on Computing in Education 25(3), 303-26

"...students at the distance classroom had a significantly more positive attitude than students at the origination site. There was **no significant difference** in the average grades earned by the students at the two sites."

1993

Jurasek, K. A.
Distance Education via Compressed Video: An Evaluation of the Attitudes and Perceptions of Students and Instructors
Iowa State University; Ames, IA

"...in the French IV class...**no difference** was found between the traditionally taught students and all DE students...There was **no difference** found in or mean final grade between the traditional class and the DE-primary class."

1993

Knott, T. D.
Distance Education Effectiveness
U. S. Distance Learning Association ED
Journal, 7-16

"The results of this study of secondary science students enrolled in an academic honors program indicate that **neither** student achievement nor attitude is **adversely affected** by distance delivery."

1993

Martin, E. D. & Rainey, L.
Student Achievement and Attitude in a Satellite-Delivered High School Science Course
The American Journal of Distance Education,
Vol. 7, No. 1

"... increased learner interaction is **not an inherently** or self-evidently **positive educational** goal or strategy."

1993

May, S.
Collaborative Learning: More is Not Necessarily Better
The American Journal of Distance Education,
Vol. 7 (3), 39-50

"Multimedia is **at least as effective** as conventional forms..."

1993

Regan, T., Boyce, M., Redwine, D., Savenye, W. C. , McMichael, J.
Is Multimedia Worth It?: A Review of the Effectiveness of Individualized Multimedia Instruction
A paper presented at the Association for Educational Communications and Technology Convention; New Orleans, LA

"...group-based multimedia can be **as effective** as individualized multimedia, and it can be **as effective** or more so than traditional forms of instruction ...unable to predict which situations are appropriate for group-based multimedia, and that it would be erroneous to state that group-based multimedia is always superior to traditional instruction or individualized multimedia."

"This study has shown that distance learners can **perform as well as** or better than traditional learners in management of technology master's degree programs, as measured by exams, term papers, and homework assignments. Thus, this study adds to the burgeoning evidence that distance learners should not be viewed as disadvantaged..."

"Participants in the IVN workshop learned marketing concepts **as well** as those in the regular workshop."

"...the on-line education programs at the University of Phoenix are proving to be **equally as effective** (and in many cases, more so) as the real-time classes taught on campus."

1993

Smith, P. L., Hsu, S., Azzarello, J., McMichael, J.
Group-Based Multimedia: Research Conclusions and Future Question
A paper presented at the Association for Educational Communications and Technology Convention; New Orleans, LA

1993

Souder, W. E.
The Effectiveness of Traditional vs. Satellite Delivery in Three Management of Technology Master's Degree Programs
The American Journal of Distance Education, Vol. 7, No. 1

1994

Flaskerud, G.
The Effectiveness of An Interactive Video Network IVN Extension Workshop
DEOSNEWS Vol. 4, No. 9, ISSN 1062-9406
Pennsylvania State University; University Park, PA

1994

Gerhing, G.
A Degree Program Offered Entirely On-Line: Does It Work?
Tel-Ed '94 Conference Proceedings, 104-106

"...comprehension and terminology were **not significantly different**...the generative nature of manipulating the visuals showed **no significant** main effect...means were higher for the cued organization, although **not significantly**, than the control."

1994

Haag, B. B. & Grabowski, B. L.
The Effects of Varied Visual Organizational Strategies Within Computer-Based Instruction on Factual, Conceptual and Problem Solving Learning
A paper presented at the Association for Educational Communications and Technology Convention; Memphis, TN

"The results of this study support the original hypothesis that there would be **no significant difference** among the students taking distance education courses...there really is **no significant difference** between the remote and non-remote groups."

1994

McGreal, R.
Comparison of the Attitudes of Learners Taking Audiographic Teleconferencing Courses in Secondary Schools in Northern Ontario
Interpersonal Computing & Technology:
An Electronic Journal for the 21st Century,
11-23

"...there were **no significant differences** in posttest performance between the adaptive and nonadaptive groups..."

1994

Mory, E. H.
The Use of Response Certitude in Adaptive Feedback Effects on Student Performance, Feedback Study Time, and Efficiency
Journal of Educational Computing Research
11(3)

"...89% of the employers considered the performance of CCHS (primarily print-based) graduates to be the "**same**" or "better" than that of graduates of other programs (classroom-based)."

1994

Scheiderman, K.
Respiratory Therapy Technician Program: Evaluation of Technical Program
(unpublished)
California College for Health Sciences;
National City, CA

"...students **learn equally well** from lessons delivered with any medium, face-to-face or at a distance...hundreds of media comparison studies that indicated, unequivocally, that there is **no inherent significant difference** in the educational effectiveness of media...Further comparison of the effectiveness were not needed. The specific medium does not matter...Students learning at a distance have the potential to learn **just as much and as well** as students taught traditionally."

1994

Schlosser, C. A., Anderson, M. L.
Distance Education: Review of the Literature
Research Institute for Studies in Education
Iowa State University; Ames, IA

68

"In the minds of the distance learning professional, at least, sufficient evidence exists to affirm that teaching via media **does no violence** to teaching. The media is a mere vehicle and successful learning comes from other factors related to learners, support, course design, motivation, and need. We have gone beyond the initial phase of using media to teach students at a distance, during which we had to demonstrate over and over again that teachers could teach and students could learn... Studies of media preference are common in comparing face-to-face instruction to telephone-based instruction. In general, there are **no differences** in preferred media. When faced with the option of traveling to a live class, students prefer learning by telephone."

1994

Threlkeld, R., Brzoska, K.
Research in Distance Education
B. Willis (Ed.) Distance Education: Strategies and Tools (41-66)
Educational Technology Publications

"All studies in the table reported **no significant differences** between resident and distant groups. It appears from the studies reviewed here that student achievement in distance learning courses is **comparable** to student achievement in resident courses… Studies conducted in military settings tend to show **no significant difference** in achievement between distance learners and resident learners..."

"There is **no significant difference** between the campus-based students and the distance learners in terms of final course grades."

"In looking at how interesting the course content was, the differences among delivery modes are **not significant**...results (grades) support the hypothesis of **equal** or better performance. Some preliminary results for all courses showed **no significant differences**...Once again, as for the combined results, there are **no statistically significant differences**..."

1995

Barry, M. & Runyan, G.   A Review of *Distance-Learning Studies in the U.S. Military*
The American Journal of Distance Education
9(3): 37-47

1995

Dexter, D. J.
Student Performance-Based Outcomes of Televised Interactive Community College
Distance Education, Doctoral dissertation
Colorado State University; Fort Collins, CO

1995

Hiltz, S. R.
Impacts of College-Level Courses via Asynchronous Learning Networks:
Focus on Students
Sloan Conference on Asynchronous Learning Networks; Philadelphia, PA

"Results showed **no significant difference** in math achievement among the three groups. There were also **no differences** in student attitudes toward enrolling in future ITV courses when comparing the host site with the remote site…The results of this study show that in developmental algebra students at the distance learning sites are learning **as well** as those students in the traditional classrooms."

"Based on an analysis of the statistical results reported in Chapter 3, ANG NCO Academy Seminar Program students perform **as well** as their resident NCO Academy counter-parts and are more positive about their NCO Academy experience. Specifically, there is **no statistical difference** in student achievement as measured by the cumulative phase test scores or the communication skills (speaking and writing) exercises between students in the ANG Seminar Programs' teleseminar environment and students in the resident NCO Academies. It is interesting that there was **no difference** between the ANG Seminar student performance on phase test 3 and their in-residence counterparts when the instruction for all groups was delivered in an in-residence environment."

"…off-campus students were compared to on-campus students… **Neither** group was significantly different from the other on their pre-test performance. The same is true of both groups on the objective post-test measure. The t-test revealed no significant difference between the groups…"

1995

Hodge-Hardin, S. L.
Interactive Television in the Classroom: A Comparison of Student Math Achievement Among Three Instructional Settings
Doctoral Dissertation
East Tennessee State University; Johnson City, TN

1995

Hunter, B., Renckly, T., Smith, J., Tussey, D.
The Effects on Student Achievement and Attitudes of a Distance Learning Seminar Educational Program Compared to a Traditional in-Residence Program
Washington, D. C.: Air University,
Air Education and Training Command
U.S. Air Force

1995

McCleary, I. D. & Egan, M. W.
Program Design and Evaluation: Two-way Interactive Television
Readings in Distance Education, Number 4
Video-based Telecommunication in Distance Education
Pennsylvania State University; University Park, PA

"Analysis of scores of math achievement test measuring the objectives of the lessons revealed that assignment to the two CBI delivery modes did not have a significant effect on the overall comprehension and learning mastery of the related mathematical materials. No significant differences between the lower-ability students across the two treatment groups were observed...Overall there were no significant differences between the two main treatment groups."

"...there are generally **no differences** in achievement between students in traditional classes and those in distance delivered classes, or between distance students at remote sites and those at origination sites where a teacher is present."

"This study has shown that distance learners can perform **as well as** or better than traditional learners in management of technology master's degree programs, as measured by exams, term papers, and homework assignments."

"Analysis of examination scores for nine semesters indicates that professionals participating from the worksite performed at a level that was generally **not statistically discernable** (at the 5% level) from the performance of students at the UW-Madison (campus)...the performance of students at remote sites is generally comparable to that of students in the classroom."

1995

Rehaag, D. M. and Szabo, M.
An Experiment on Effects of Redundant Audio in Computer-Based Instruction on Achievement, Attitude, and Learning Time in Tenth-Grade Math
A paper presented at the Association for Educational Communications and Technology Conference in Anaheim, California, February

1995

Sorensen, C. K.
Evaluation of Two-Way Interactive Television for Community College Instruction
ACEC Conference; Ames, Iowa

1995

Souder, W. E.
The Effectiveness of Traditional vs. Satellite Delivery in Three Management of Technology Master's Degree Programs
Readings in Distance Education, No. 4
Video-Based Telecommunication in Distance Education
Pennsylvania State University; University Park, PA

1996

Davis, J. L.
Computer-Assisted Distance Learning, Part II: Examination Performance of Students On & Off Campus
Journal of Engineering Education, Jan. 77-82

"...a large majority of respondents rated distance instruction as **equal** to or better than face-to-face instruction."

1996

Franks, K.
Attitudes of Alaskan Distance Education Students Toward Media and Instruction
The American Journal of Distance Education
Vol. 10, No. 3, 60-71

"Studies of computer-mediated education in university settings do not find they 'speed up' learning or make students 'perform better'. Typically, evaluation studies find **no difference** with traditional education."

1996

Garson, G. D.
The Political Economy of Online Education
(unpublished paper)
North Carolina State University; Raleigh, NC

"Students that had access to only WWW-based material or the lectures performed **roughly the same**. It is encouraging that it seems possible for a WWW-based offering to be as effective as a traditional lecture-based course."

1996

Goldberg, M. W.
CALOS: First Results From an Experiment in Computer-Aided Learning
University of British Columbia, Canada

"...the academic performance of \students in the program was **equal** to or better than that of its classroom-based students in both quantitative and non-quantitative areas."

1996

Hedegaard, T.
Computer-Mediated Online Education: Lessons Learned by the University of Phoenix
ED Journal (February) Vol. 10 No. 2

"...many individual studies have shown **no significant differences** between modes of delivery. **No one medium** emerged as consistently **better or worse** in delivering information to students."

1996

Krendl, K. A., Ware, W. H., Reid, K. A., Warren, R.
Learning by Any Other Name: Communication Research Traditions in Learning and Media
Handbook of Research for Educational Communications and Technology, D. H. Jonassen, ed. Macmillan, 93-111

"One reason why online education is 'supposed' to be less expensive education in the minds of many administrators is because evaluation studies do **not** show it to be **pedagogically more effective**..."

"Much traditional research in distance education has focused on issues of technology...most of those related to technology were media comparison studies that resulted in **no significant difference**."

"...there is **little reliable evidence** (yet) to **support the claims** that hypertext systems can really support alternative and superior modes of learning."

"Comparing the achievement of learners (as measured by grades, test scores, retention, job performance) who are taught at a distance and those taught in face-to-face classes is a line of research going back more than 50 years. The usual finding in these comparison studies is that there are **no significant differences** between learning in the two different environments, regardless of the nature of the content, the educational level of the students, or the media involved...reasonable to conclude...

(continued on next page)

1996

McClure, P. A.
Technology Plans and Measurable Outcomes
Educom Review, (May/June) Vol. 31, No. 3, 29-30

1996

McIsaac, M. S., Gunawardena, C. N.
Hard Technologies: Media-Related Research 13, Distance Education
Handbook of Research for Educational Communications and Technology, D. H. Jonassen, ed. Macmillan, 403-37

73

1996

McKnight, C., Dillon, A., Richardson, J.
User-Centered Design of Hypertext/Hypermedia for Education
Handbook of Research for Educational Communications and Technology, D. H. Jonassen, ed. Macmillan, 622-33

1996

Moore, M. G., Kearsley, G.
Research on Effectiveness
Chapter 4 - Distance Education: A Systems View Wadsworth Publishing, ISBN 0-534-26496-4

... (continued from previous page)

1. there is insufficient evidence to support the idea that classroom instruction is the optimum delivery method.

2. instruction at a distance can be as effective in bringing about learning as classroom instruction.

3. the absence of face-to-face contact is not in itself detrimental to the learning process.

4. what makes any course good or poor is a consequence of how well it is designed, delivered, and conducted, not whether the students are face-to-face or at a distance."

"There were **no significant differences** found, even though the trends of scores were similar to those obtained from the original administration of the attitude test...There was **no significant difference** found between subjects categorized as being either field dependent or field independent, nor was there a significant interaction between field dependence and treatment."

"Results of the study indicated **no significant differences** between the three groups in regard to student/teacher interaction or course structure."

1996

Simonson, M. & Maushak, N.
Instructional Strategies Research 34
Instructional Technology and Attitude Change
Handbook of Research for Educational Communications and Technology, D. H. Jonassen, ed. Macmillan, 984-1016

1996

Thomerson, J. D. & Smith, C. L.
Student Perceptions of the Affective Experiences Encountered in Distance Learning Courses
The American Journal of Distance Education Vol. 10, No. 3, 37-58

"...auditory presentations can be **at least as effective** as live or print presentations and are practical alternatives to conventional instruction...radio instruction has been found to be **at least as effective** as conventional instruction... In general, comparisons of learning from audio and print have shown **no difference**."

"On the whole, results have been mixed, but instructional treatments under the learner's control have been shown most often to be **as effective** or less effective than treatments under more computer control...Most studies, however, found **no difference** overall between learner-controlled and program-controlled treatments. The various conclusions drawn from this '**no difference**" findings are interesting and tend to reflect a good deal of rationalization."

"Grades and performance of the online learners proved **neither better nor worse** on the average than traditional section students."

"...the average grades of Fountain Valley classes were **marginally** to half-a-grade **better** than those of their campus-bound counterparts."

1996

Tripp, S. D. & Roby, W. B.
Instructional Message Design Research 28.
Auditory Presentations and Language
Laboratories
Handbook of Research for Educational
Communications and Technology, D. H.
Jonassen, ed. Macmillan, 821-50

1996

Williams, M. D.
Instructional Strategies Research 33
Learner-Control and Instructional Technologies
Handbook of Research for Educational
Communications and Technology, D. H.
Jonassen, ed. Macmillan 957 83

1996

Wilson, D. L.
Self-Paced Studies
Chronicle of Higher Education, Vol. XLII, No.
21, Feb. 2, A19-A201996

1996

Witherspoon, J. P. A
"2+2" Baccalaureate Program Using Interactive
Video
DEOSNEWS Vol. 6, No. 6, ISSN 1062-9416
Pennsylvania State University; University
Park, PA

"Analysis of pretest measures by single factor completely randomized ANOVAs showed **nonsignificant differences**... There were **nonsignificant differences** between the workshop and CBA groups, and between the control and CBA groups."

"With regard to student learning, there was **no statistical difference** in performance between the students at the different locations."

"The research (good or bad) says that there is **no significant difference** (between any method and any other method)."

"...there can be no doubt that motivated cyberstudents can learn **as well** as motivated on-site students."

"The University banks, whose funding model discourages large classes, initially penalized the college of business for TV teaching, even though TV students test as well as those in conventional classes."

"Extensive research findings indicate that **no direct link has been established** between delivery medium, levels of interaction, and the of both on student achievement..."

1997

Beaman, I., O'Connell, B., Smyrnios, K.
The Value of Enhancing Accounting Knowledge Using Computer-Based Learning Approaches
Monash University, Australia

1997

Brawner, C. E.
North Carolina State: Fujitsu Network Based Education Project Course Evaluation Report
Electronically published
<http://www3.ncsu.edu/dox/NBE/brawner/course_eval.html>

1997

Ehrmann, S., Greenburg, J.
Does Technology Really Make Students Learn Better? (Interview)
American Association for Higher Education (AAHE) Listserve, June 10

1997

Gubernick, L. & Ebeling, A.
I Got My Degree Through E-mail
Forbes, June 16

1997

Hammonds, K. H., and Jackson, S.
The New University: A Tough Market is Reshaping Colleges
Business Week, December 22

1997

Keast, David A.
Toward an Effective Model for Implementing Distance Education Programs
The American Journal of Distance Education
Vol.11 no.2

"The performance of the web based students is **equal** to that of my traditional class room students."

"Most of the distance education research has found that students in well-designed DE courses perform **as well** as students in well-designed traditional courses."

"**No significant difference** was found in scores between on-campus and distance students."

"**No statistically significant difference** in grades in either course."

"...students **learn as much** in telephone teaching as they do in video or face-to-face instruction..."

1997

Marsh, J.
Anyone Doing Research on the Pedagogy?
The Distance Education Online Symposium
November 5

1997

Martin, B., Moskal, P., Foshee, N., Morse, L
So You Want to Develop a Distance Education Course?
American Society for Engineering Education
(ASEE) PRISM, February

1997

Martin, S.
Georgia Statewide Academic and Medical System Two-Way Interactive Audio and Video System Experience
The Distance Education Online Symposium
posting, January 16

1997

Miller, T., Hewitt, K. & Brawner, C.
Distance Teaching Over the Internet Multicast Backbone
A paper presented at the Instructional Technologies Exposition, September
North Carolina State University; Raleigh, NC

1997

Olgren, C. H.
Teaching by Telephone
Teaching and Learning at a Distance: What It Takes to Effectively Design, Deliver, and Evaluate Programs, T. E. Cyrs, ed. Jossey-Bass Publishers, 60

"This research encompasses elementary through graduate education, and includes military, government, business and individual training... these studies have concluded there is **no significant differences** in achievement between learners being taught via instructional television, whether in a remote or classroom location, and learners being taught face-to-face with the instructor...The research findings on student achievement using instructional television are clear. The weight of the evidence shows students in instructional television courses learn **as much**, or in some cases, more than, their counterparts in traditional, face-to-face courses. Therefore, students participating in telecourses can be expected to do **as well** in achievement as they would have done in a traditionally delivered course, and should not be considered to be at a disadvantage..."

"**No significant differences** were found in final course grades between web-based sections and classroom-based sections. This finding also held true when prior grade-point average (GPA) was taken into account. **No significant differences** were found by gender in the performance of students in undergraduate web-based sections."

"...we find from our research that web-based classes perform **as well as** face-to-face classes."

1997

Payne, H. E.
A Review of the Literature: Interactive Video in Distance Learning Courses
Ed Journal, Vol.11 no.10, j1-16

1998

Hoey, J. J., Pettitt, J. M., Brawner, C. E.,
*Project 25: First-Semester Assessment—
A Report on the Implementation of Courses Offered on the Internet*
North Carolina State University; Raleigh, NC

1998

Sechrest, J.,
The Internet Is An Educational Medium
WWW Courseware Development Literature
<www.dev@listserv.uiub.CA> April 20

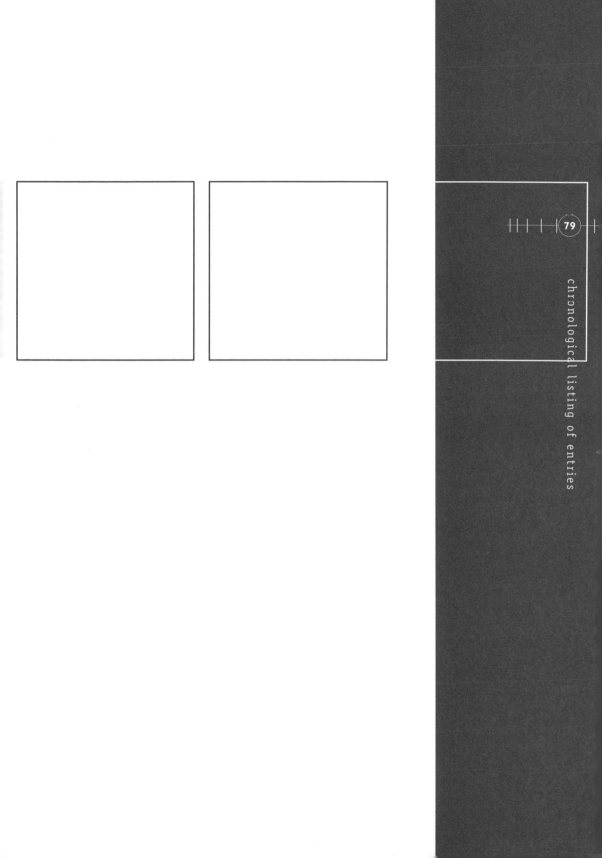

new
entries

The AT&T Communications National Teletraining Network: Applications, Benefits and Costs	Chute, A.G., Burning, K.K., Hulick, M.K. 1984
Addressing Vocational Training and Retraining Through Educational Technology: Policy Alternatives	Herschback, D. 1984
Adult Education and Vocational Education: Implications for Research on Distance Delivery	McClelland, J., Saeed, F. 1986
Anyone Doing Research on the Pedagogy?	Marsh, J. 1997
Attitudes of Alaskan Distance Education Students Toward Media and Instruction	Franks, K. 1996
Audio-Tutorial Approach to Learning	Postlethwaite, S.N., Novak, J., Murray, H.T. 1972
Closed Circuit Television: Teaching in Washington County	Hagerstown: The Board of Education 1959
Collaborative Learning: More is Not Necessarily Better	May, S. 1993
Comments on "Language Laboratory Research: A Critique"	Lorge, S.W. 1965
Communication Modality as a Determinant of Message Persuasiveness and Message Comprehensibility	Chaiken, S., Egly, A. 1976
A Comparison of Movie and Multi-Image Presentation Techniques on Affective and Cognitive Learning	Atherton, L.L. 1971
A Comparison of Phonographic Recordings with Printed Material in Terms of Knowledge	Rulon, P.V. 1943
A Comparison of Phonographic Recordings with Printed Material in Terms of Knowledge Gained Through Their Use as a Teaching Unit	Rulon, P.V. 1943
A Comparison of Phonographic Recordings with Printed Motivation to Further Study	Rulon, P.V. 1943
Comparison of Student Performance and Attitude Under Three Lesson-Selection Strategies in Computer-Assisted Instruction	Beard, M.H., Lorton, P.V., Searle, B.W., Atkinson, R.C 1973

Comparison of the Cognitive and Affective Responses of College Students to Single-Image and Multi-Image Audio-Visual Presentations	Didcoct, D.H. 1958
Computer-Assisted Distance Learning, Part II: Examination Performance of Students On and Off Campus	Davis, J.L. 1996
Computer-Based Instruction Delivery Systems	Tso, A. 1988
Computer-Mediated Online Education: Lessons Learned by the University of Phoenix	Hedgegaard, T. 1996
Control of Feedback in Computer-Assisted Instruction	Pridemore, D.R., Klein, J.D. 1991
Distance Education: Learning Outcomes, Interaction and Attitudes	Haynes, J.M., Dillon, C. 1992
Distance Teaching Over the Internet Multicast Backbone	Miller, T., Hewitt, K., Brawner, C. 1997
Does Technology Really Make Students Learn Better?	Ehrmann, S., Greenberg, J. 1997
The Effect of a Student Response Systems Questions on Learner Attention and Performance in a Distance Learning Environment	Garvin-Kester, B. J. 1990
Effect of Adjunct Postquestions on Achievement	Sutliff, R. 1986
The Effect of Delay of Informative Feedback on the Retention of Verbal Information and Higher-Order Learning for College Students	Char, R.O. 1978
The Effect of Delayed Comparison in the Language Laboratory on Phoneme Discrimination and Pronouncement Accuracy	Sisson, C.R. 1970
The Effect of Immediacy and Type of Informative Feedback on Retention in a Computer-Assisted Task	Wager, S.U. 1983
The Effect of Large-Screen Multi-Image Display of Evaluation Meaning	Bollman, C.G. 1970
The Effect of Type of Feedback on Rule Learning in Computer-Based Instruction	Lee, O.M. 1985

The Effectiveness of Telecommunications as an Educational Delivery System	Hoyt, D.P., Frye, D. 1972
The Effectiveness of the Audio-Laboratory in Elementary Modern Language Courses	Brushwood, J., Polmantier, P. 1953
The Effects of Computer-Mediated Text on Measures of Reading Comprehension and Reading Behavior	Reinking, D., Schreiner, R. 1985
The Effects of Cooperative Learning Strategies on Achievement and Attitudes During Interactive Video	Dalton, D.W. 1990
Effects of Educational Setting on Student Responses to Structured Hypertext	van den Berg, S. Watt, J.H. 1991
The Effects of Four Methods of Immediate Feedback on Retention, Discrimination Error, and Feedback Study Time in Computer-based Instruction	Dempsey, J.V. 1988
The Effects of Learning of Structural Drills in Spanish Broadcast via High Frequency AM Radio	Cook, H.R. 1964
The Effects of University Television Instruction and Factors Influencing Student Attitude	Hult, TR. E. 1980
The Effects of Varied Visual Organizational Strategies Within Computer-Based Instruction on Factual, Conceptual and Problem-Solving Learning	Haag, B.B, Grabowski, B.L. 1994
Effects on Childrens' Achievement and Curiosity of Variations in Learner Control Over an Interactive Video Lesson	Armone, M.P., Grabowski, B.L. 1992
The Effects on Student Achievement and Attitudes of a Distance Learning Seminar Educational Program Compared to a Traditional In-Residence Program	Hunter, B., Renckly, T., Smith, J., Tussey, D. 1995
Empirical Issues in the Study of Computer-Assisted Interactive Video	Hannafin, M.J. 1985

An Evaluation of Telecourse Achievement at Saddleback College	Smith, J. 1984
An Evaluation of the Spitz Student Response System in Teaching a Course in Logical and Mathematical Concepts	Brown, J.D. 1972
An Experiment on Effects of Redundant Audio in Computer-Based Instruction on Achievement, Attitude and Learning Time in Tenth-Grade Math	Rehaag, D.M., Szabo, M. 1995
Failure to Increase Learning Using The Time Saved by the Time Compression of Speech	Sticht, T.G. 1971
The Feasibility of Using Taped Lectures to Replace Class Attendance	Menne, J.W., Klingenschmidt, J.E., Nord, D.L. 1969
Feedback, Retention, Discrimination Error, and Feedback Study Time	Dempsey, J.V., Driscoll, M.P., Litchfield, B.C. 1993
Further Research on Speeded Speech as an Educational Mediu—the Use of Listening Aids	Friedman, H.L., Orr, D., Norris, C. 1966
Georgia Statewide Academic and Medical System Two-Way Interactive Audio and Video System Experience	Martin, S. 1997
Group-Based Multimedia: Research Conclusions and Future Question	Smith, P.L., Hsu, S., Azzarello, J., McMichael, J. 1993
Hard Technologies: Media-Related Research 13. Distance Education	McIsaac, M.S., Gunawardena, C.N. 1996
I Got My Degree Through E-mail	Gubernick, L., Ebeling, A. 1997
Incidental Learning During Information Retrieval: A Hypertext Experiment	Jones, T. 1989
Instructional Film Reports, Vol. 2	Carpenter, C.R., Greenhill, L.P. 1956
Instructional Media Research: Past, Present and Future	Allen, W.H. 1971
Instructional Message Design Research 28, Auditory Presentations and Language Laboratories	Tripp, S.D., Roby, W.B. 1996

Instructional Strategies Research 33, Learner-Control and Instructional Technologies	Williams, M.D. 1996
Instructional Strategies Research 34, Instructional Technology Attitude Change	Simonson, M., Maushak, N. 1996
Instructional Television as a Medium of Teaching in Higher Education	Judd, W.A., Bunderson, C.V., Bessent, E.W. 1970
Interactive Distance Education in Higher Education and the Impact of Delivery Styles on Student Perceptions	Britton, O.L. 1992
The Internet Is An Educational Medium	Sechrest, J. 1998

An Investigation of the Interaction Between the Level of Meaningfulness and Redundancy in the Content of the Stimulus Material, and the Mode of Presentation of the Stimulus Material	VanMondfrans, A.P. 1963
Is Multimedia Worth It?: A Review of the Effectiveness of Individualized Multimedia Instruction	Regan, T., Boyce, M., Redwine, D., Savenye, W.C., McMichael, J. 1993
Language Learning and Frequency Response	Buka, M., Freeman, M.K., Locke, W.N. 1962
Language Learning Laboratory	Smith, W.F. 1970
Learner Control and Achievement in Science Computer-Assisted Instruction	Kinzie, M.B., Sullivan, H.J. 1988
Learner Control of Computer-Assisted Instruction: A Comparison to Guided Instruction	Lahey, G.F. 1978
Learner Control Versus Program Control in Interactive Videodisc Instruction: What Are The Effects in Procedural Learning?	Shyu, H.-Y., Brown, S.W. 1992
Learning by Any Other Name: Communication Research Traditions in Learning and Media	Krendl, K.A., Ware, W.H., Reid, K.A., Warren, R. 1996
Listening Effect of Radio English Classroom	NHK Radio - Television Cultural Research Institute 1956

Media and Instructional Methods	Winn, B. 1990
Methods	Lange, D.L. 1968
Multi-channel, Multi-image Teaching of Synthesis Skills in Eleventh-Grade U. S. History	Lombard, E.S. 1969
The New University: A Tough Market is Reshaping Colleges	Hammonds, K.H., Jackson, S. 1997
North Carolina State: Fujitsu Network-Based Education Project Course Evaluation Report	Brawner, C.E. 1997
Pictures, Audio, and Print: Symbolic Representation and Effect on Learning	Nugent, G.C. 1982
Problems in Instructional Television in Latin America	Tiffon, J.W. 1978
Project 25: First Semester Assessment—A Report on the Implementation of Courses on the Internet	Hoey, J.J., Pettit, J.M., Brauner, C.E. 1998
Purdue Laboratory Method in Teaching Beginning Classes	Fotos, J.T. 1955
Radio in the Elementary School	Constantine, M. 1964
Relationship Between Learner Control of CA1 and Locus of Control Among Hispanic Students	Lopez, C.L., Harper, M. 1989
Relative Effectiveness of Instruction of Films Exclusively, Films Plus Study Guides, and Standard Lecture Methods	VanderMeer, A.W. 1950
Research on Telecommunicated Learning: Past, Present and Future	Johnstone, S.M. 1991
A Review of the Literature: Interactive Video in Distance Learning Courses	Payne, H.E. 1997
Review of Trends in Research on Instructional Television and Film	Greenhill, L.P. 1967
Simulteaching: Access to Learning by Means of Interactive Television	Nixon, D.E. 1992

new entries

Single and Multi-Channel Communication: A Review of Research and a Proposed Model AV	Hartman, F.R. 1961
So You Want to Develop a Distance Education Course?	Martin, B., Moskal, P., Foshee, N., Morse, L. 1997
Spartanburg, S.C.: Testing the Effectiveness of Video, Voice and Data Feedback	Lucas, W.A. 1978
Student Perceptions of the Affective Experiences Encountered in Distance Learning Courses	Thomerson, J.D., Smith, C.L. 1996
A Study of Aural Learning With and Without the Speaker Present	Loder, J.E. 1937
Tape Recorded Lectures in the College Classroom II	Popham, W.J. 1962
Teaching by Telephone	Olgren, C.H. 1997
Teaching Psychology by Telephone	Cutler, R.L., McKeachie, W.J., McNeil, E.B. 1958
Telecourse Students: How Well Do They Learn?	Purdy, L 1978
Televised Teaching Effectiveness: Two Case Studies	Chung, J. 1991
Television Research in the Teaching Learning Process	Holmes, P.D. 1959
Theory of Perception and the Design of Audiovisual Materials	Travers, R.M.W. 1968
Toward an Effective Model for Implementing Distance Education Programs	Keast, D.A. 1997
The Travel Metaphor as Design Principle and Training Aid for Navigating Around Complex Systems	Hammond, N., Allison, L. 1989
The Use of Interactive Television in Business Education	Pirrong, G.D., Lathen, W.G. 1990
The Use of Response Certitude in Adaptive Feedback Effects on Student Performance, Feedback Study Time, and Efficiency	Mory, E.H. 1994
User-Centered Design of Hypertext/Hypermedia for Education	McKnight, C., Dillon, A., Richardson, J. 1996

Using Elaboration Strategies Training in Computer-Based Instruction to Promote Generative Learning

Johnsey, A., Morrison, G.R., Ross, S.M.
1992

The Value of Enhancing Accounting Knowledge Using Computer-Based Learning Approaches

Beaman, I., O'Connell, B., Smyrnios, K.
1997

What Is The Scientific Value of Comparing Automated and Human Instruction?

Hoko, A.
1986

new entries

index by principal researchers/authors

index by principal researchers/authors

index by
techno-
logy/var
iations

index by technology/variations

year

index by technology/variations

index by technology/variations

biblio-
graphy

Clark, Richard E. (1994) **Media will never influence learning.**
Educational Technology Research and Development 42 (2), 21-29.

____1983, **Reconsidering Research on Learning from Media.**
Review of Research, Vol. 53, No. 4, 445-49.

Cuban, L. (1986) **Teachers and Machines:**
The Classroom Use of Technology since 1920.
Teachers College Press, New York.

Heinrich, Robert (1984) **The Proper Study of Instructional Technology.**
Educational Communications and Technology Journal, Vol. 32, No. 2, 67-87.

Holmberg, Robert G., & Bakshi, Trilochan S. (1992) **Postmortem on a Distance Education**
Course: Successes and Failures.
The American Journal of Distance Education, Vol. 6, No. 1, 27-39.

Jacobson, Robert L. (1993) **As Instructional Technology Proliferates, Skeptics**
Seek Hard Evidence of Its Value.
The Chronicle of Higher Education, May 5, A27-29.

____(1994) **The Coming Revolution.**
The Chronicle of Higher Education, April 27, p. A26.

Jonassen, David H., editor. **Handbook of Research for Educational Communications**
and Technology. 1996.

Lombardi, John V. (1994) **Campuses Need Not Wait for Snazzy New Technology**
to Enter Cyberspace.
The Chronicle of Higher Education, Vol. XL, No. 26, p. A48.

"The Medium Ain't the Message" (1997) Editors of *Training*, September, p. 26.

Murray, F. (1983) **Cognitive benefits of teaching on the teacher.**
Paper presented at American Educational Research Association Annual Meeting,
Montreal, Quebec.

Oppenheimer, Todd (1997) **The Computer Delusion.**
The Atlantic Monthly, Vol. 280, No. 1, 45-62.

Pittman, Von (1997) **Distance Education Exchange.**
Journal of Continuing Higher Education, Vol. 45, No. 2, Spring, 42-43.

Russell, Thomas L. (1993) **Comparative Research Response/Rebuttal.**
Research in Distance Education, Vol. 5, Nos. 1 & 2, January/April, 5.

____(1995) **Distance Education: How High the Tech?**
Proceedings: Distance Education: Sharing the Experience II, Portland, OR., March 1-4, 52-4.

____(1994) **Interactivity versus Virtual Interactivity:
Which Does The Research Support?**
*Proceedings for Tel^Ed '94: The Third International Symposium on Telecommunications
in Education*, Albuquerque, NM, Nov. 10-13, 251-54.

____(1997) **Technology Wars: Winners & Losers.**
Educom Review, Vol. 32, No. 2, March/April, 44-6.

____(1996) **Technology's Threat to the Traditional Institution: Real or Imagined?**
ACHE (Association for Continuing Higher Education), *The Journal of Continuing Higher
Education*, Vol. 44, No. 1, Winter, pp. 22-4.

Schlosser, Charles A. & Anderson, Mary L. (1994) **Distance Education:
Review of the Literature.**
Association for Educational Communications and Technology, Washington, 64.

Schubin, Mark (1994) **Tomorrow's A Day Away.**
Videography, Vol. 19, No. 9, 18-54.

Van Haalen, Teresa & Miller, George (1994) **Interactivity as a Predictor
of Student Success in Satellite Learning Programs.**
Deosnews, Vol. 4, No. 6.

bibliography

about the author

Thomas L. Russell is the director of the Office of Instructional Telecommunications at North Carolina State University where he provides both leadership for and management of the university's distance education activities. His career, spanning more than 40 years, includes teaching—elementary through university levels—instructional television production, research, and distance education. He has published 64 articles and provided almost 200 seminars, conference presentations, and workshops in many parts of the world.

In 1976 Mr. Russell proposed and developed the first technology-based distance education system at North Carolina State University. This system continues to successfully meet the needs for which it was devised in addition to reaching out to other institutions in the United States and abroad. The current incarnation of this endeavor, the VideoClass System which employs unique applications of television and computer technologies, has been put into operation by Mr. Russell at North Carolina State University, in other parts of the United States, and in India, Peru, South Africa and Sweden.

As a consultant, Mr. Russell assists both domestic and foreign institutions as well as business and government agencies to fulfill their distance education and distance training needs in an affordable and timely manner.

DISCARD